Murder in Gales

A Rose Hanged Twice

Patricia Lubeck

outskirtspress

DENVER, COLORADO

Outskirts Press, Inc.
http://www.outskirtspress.com

ISBN: 978-1-4327-9129-2

Outskirts Press and the "OP" logo are trademarks belonging to Outskirts Press, Inc.

PRINTED IN THE UNITED STATES OF AMERICA

Acknowledgments

There are so many people to thank for helping me write this story. First, I would like to give much gratitude to my friend and research specialist, Michelle Gatz. She devoted many hours in gathering material, contacting agencies, and locating descendants for information and photos. Her perseverance and inspiration were my motivation to write this book.

A special thank you to historical societies in Minnesota who provided information or photos that helped tell this story: Darla Gebhard, Brown County Historical Society; Ellayne Conyers, Lyon County Historical Society; Char Larson, Murray County Historical Society; Debbie Joramo, Sleepy Eye Area Historical Society; Doris Weber, Springfield Area Historical Society; Gary Revier, Redwood County Historical Society; and Jan Louwagie, Southwest Minnesota State University. A very special thank you to staff at the Redwood Falls Public Library who provided numerous rolls of microfilm for my perusal.

I would also like to express my gratitude to family descendants who were willing to share personal histories and photographs that contributed immensely in bringing this story to life. This book could not have been written without the support and inspiration of so many people. My sincere thanks to all those not mentioned who provided material and photographs included in this amazing story.

I'd like to extend a very special thank you to Joan Rogers for her expertise in editing the manuscript, and much gratitude goes to the publishing team at Outskirts Press who guided me through the extensive publishing and marketing process. I couldn't have done it without the support of this wonderful group of professionals.

Last, but certainly not least, I wish to extend heartfelt thanks to my husband, Michael, for his constant support and words of encouragement.

Table of Contents

Introduction

In the early days when the prairie was a wide expanse of tall grasses, wildflowers, and roaming herds of buffalo, the promise of free land brought thousands of Americans living in the East to settle in the western states. Immigrants from Europe left their homelands in hopes of owning a piece of land in America, all sharing the dream of finding a new and better life.

The Homestead Act, offering the opportunity for free land, was passed and signed into law by Abraham Lincoln in May 1862. To qualify for homestead rights to a 160-acre parcel of land, one had to be head of household or at least 21 years of age. The law instituted a threefold acquisition process.

First, one had to go to the nearest land office, complete an application, and submit a $10 filing fee, plus a $2 commission, to the land agent to claim temporary occupation of the land. Secondly, he had to improve the land by building a 12 x 14 dwelling and grow crops, both required for "proving up"; and lastly, file for deed of title at the end of five years.

After five years, the homesteader was ready for legal possession of the land. He had to find two neighbors or friends willing to vouch for his statements of land improvements and sign a document of proof, along with paying a $6 fee to obtain the deed of title for the land.

Local land offices forwarded the paperwork to the General Land Office in Washington, DC, along with a certificate of eligibility. The case file was examined, and valid claims were granted patent to the land free and clear, except for the small registration fee.

Title could also be acquired after a six-month residency and minimal improvements, provided the claimant paid the government $1.25

an acre. After the Civil War, Union soldiers could deduct the time they served from the residency requirements.

The deed of title was signed by the current President of the United States and often proudly displayed on the cabin wall to remind the occupants of all their hard work and determination.

There were land speculators that took advantage of a legislative loophole when the law's language failed to specify whether the 12 x 14 dwelling was to be built in feet or inches. The General Land Office was underfunded and unable to hire enough investigators for the widely scattered local offices. As a result, overworked and underpaid investigators were often subject to bribery.

Six months after the Homestead Act was passed, the Railroad Act was signed, and in May 1869 the railroad system stretched across the land. This new mode of transportation brought many more settlers and immigrants westward and provided access to manufactured goods such as farm tools, barbed wire for fences, linens, weapons, and even houses. At this time, the railroad conglomerates sold off excess land at inflated prices and made a bundle.[1]

The Timber Culture Act followed the Homestead Act and was passed in 1873. It was passed to prevent abuse of the original Homestead Act of 1862. It allowed homesteaders to acquire another 160 acres of land if they set aside 40 acres to grow trees. Timber was needed to sell. It was used as wood for fires and building materials. Trees also served as a windbreak to shield settlers from the fierce winds that blew across the prairie.

After planting the trees, the land could be obtained only if it was occupied by the same family for at least five years. After five years, a certificate of ownership and proof of the planted trees could be obtained for $30. Later, the amount of land set aside for trees was reduced to ten acres.[2]

In the beginning, there were few trees for building in the plains, forcing many to build homes out of sod. This shelter was called a "soddy" and made of bricks of sod weighing up to 50 pounds each. It took about an acre of prairie sod to build a one-room house.

The physical conditions of the prairie offered many challenges. In the summer, there was the threat of prairie fires. A spark of lightning would easily set the tall, dry grass ablaze as the howling wind carried the flames at a fast pace across the land, burning crops and homes.

When autumn ended, the harsh winds of winter arrived, with blizzards bringing the temperatures to 40 degrees below zero. Families were often cut off from the outside world during heavy snowstorms.

Then there were times when plagues of grasshoppers took over the land and consumed the crops. They ate everything in their path, and many farmers abandoned their land after this, thinking they would never recover from the devastation.

Women often burned buffalo chips to ward off pesky flies, gnats, and mosquitoes. Limited fuel and water supplies turned cooking and heating chores into difficult tasks.

Prairie life was physically demanding and mentally challenging, and as a result, many homesteaders did not stay on the land long enough to fulfill the claim; thus, the act of "claim jumping" was quite common. If a homesteader abandoned his claim or did not "prove up" the land within five years, another party could lay claim to that land after contacting the local land office and submitting the proper paperwork and filing fees.[3]

In spite of the many hardships the prairie presented, two families eventually settled in southwestern Minnesota in the 1870s and became neighbors. These families were the Lufkins and the Roses.

CHAPTER ONE
The Lufkin Family

James Brown Lufkin was born in 1791 in Chester, New Hampshire and his family migrated to Phillips, Maine in the early 1800s. Phillips, Maine is a tiny village nestled in the fertile wilderness valley of the Sandy River, originally known as Shadagee; from the Indian name Chatauke, meaning "Great Place." In 1817, James wedded Alice Marrow Harris.

Lufkin was a farmer, and farming was the principal occupation of this region. Life was extremely hard -- clearing the thick woods to build a cabin for shelter, and cultivating the land to yield enough annually to sustain a huge family through the winter was indeed rugged work. The most successful settlers were those who raised large families, and the Lufkin family was no exception. James and Alice had at least ten children -- one of these being Moses Lufkin, born April 17, 1831.

Being from a large family, Moses was called upon to share in the tasks of raising siblings and helping his father with all the farming activities. Due to the heavy burden these mundane tasks put upon Moses in his youth, he eventually developed a very rebellious and incorrigible nature.

Some say Moses took on some unsavory characteristics, quite similar to his father's malicious and lawless behavior. It seems Moses' father, James, was convicted of larceny in his youth and spent time in jail.

꙳

In 1860, when Moses was 29 years old, he felt it was time to settle down and raise a family. He met a beautiful woman, named Mary Susan

Mitchell, who lived nearby. They courted for quite some time and married on June 19 of that year.

It wasn't long before a daughter, Minnie, was born. She was a cute little bundle of joy, with curly black hair, and dark-brown eyes. The firstborn tends to get lots of attention, and is doted upon, until the next newborn comes along.

In the early days of the marriage, the newlyweds seemed quite happy, but tempers flared when Mary's parents stopped by to visit their granddaughter. Moses never seemed to be home when the in-laws came around, and this didn't sit well with the Mitchells. Mary's parents never really approved of the marriage, as they knew Moses to be a very unsavory character with a bad temper. They heard rumors that Moses had been inappropriate with his sister, and no one wished to associate with him.

Moses tried hard to curb his amoral behavior, but his big ego and lack of conscience always got him into trouble. He never kept a job for very long because at some point, he would get into an altercation with the boss, and end up walking off the job, never to return.

During this time, Moses did what he could to please his wife, and struggled to provide for the new family. He didn't have a steady job, and borrowed money from family and friends to get by.

By the time Moses was 30 years of age, the United States was engaged in the Civil War. Moses, motivated by a desire for adventure, the need to escape his debtors, and trouble with his wife and in-laws, enthusiastically departed to do battle for the cause, and enlisted in the military as a volunteer on September 28, 1861 in Maine Company A, 11th Regiment.

Before leaving Augusta, Moses wrote a letter to his older brother, Francis, assigning him the task of taking care of his debts while he was away. Francis Lufkin wrote the following letter to Governor Washburn in this regard:

My brother, Moses L. Lufkin, enlisted in the 11th Regiment of Infantry, leaving some debts for me to pay as fast as he sent me *money. He wrote me he had assigned me $12 a month of his wages. Encouraged, thereby, I have advanced considerable sums to his creditors, and my own creditors are now clamorous. I expected $24 from my brother, the first of this month, and it has not come yet. I am greatly strained or I would not trouble your Excellency. Can you tell me if he has assigned me any money, and if so, how am I to get it. I am told that the money will be first sent to you. If so, you can forward it by mail with the usual precaution. Signed, F.M. Lufkin.*[1]

It is unclear whether Governor Washburn ever responded to this request, and quite probable that Francis Lufkin never received any of his brother's military wages to pay the creditors that were heavy on his heels. This did not sit well with Francis, and he vowed that one day he would deal with his brother in no uncertain terms, as soon as the war was over and he returned home. But after the war, Moses never contacted Francis, and they never spoke to each other again.

In November 1861, Moses Lufkin was appointed corporal in Penvell's Company, but shortly thereafter was discharged in February 1862, due to a back injury received while jumping 17 feet from a window at Columbian Hospital.

At that time, Moses was in the hospital for a case of typhoid fever, and while sick and in a delirious state of mind, jumped out the window, resulting in a severe spinal injury, causing chronic inflammation of the spinal column for the remainder of his life.

During the war years, military hospitals were by no means clean and restful places to recuperate from injury or illness. The hospitals averaged 500 beds and were neither heated nor well-ventilated. Sanitation was of little concern. There was no regard for sterilization of instruments, and used bandages littered the floor.

Doctors moistened stitching thread with their saliva before sewing wounds, and sharpened surgical knives on the soles of their boots. The water supply was usually contaminated, and as a result, blood poisoning, tetanus, and gangrene were extremely common.

It has been estimated that the hospitals killed as many as they saved, and given their deplorable conditions, it is understandable that soldiers often dreaded being sent to the hospital.[2]

Moses returned to his family after his discharge, but Mary did not seem happy to see him. He tried his hand at farming again, but the physical tasks of this occupation aggravated his old back injury and Moses constantly complained of pain. They fought incessantly over money matters, with Mary frequently taking solace at her parents' home nearby.

By 1863, a second daughter was born, named Grace. She had dark-brown hair, big brown eyes, and weighed only 5 lbs at birth. With a new addition to the family and another mouth to feed, matrimonial bliss was short-lived, and the couple divorced later that year. Mary had grown tired of her husband's lack of support and terrible temper, and eventually deserted Moses and went to parts unknown.

At the divorce proceedings, Moses claimed that he "behaved himself toward his wife as a chaste, faithful and affectionate husband, but his wife treated him with great cruelty." Moses said of his wife, "She proved to be possessed of a reckless disposition, cunning, deceitful and artful, either is insane or possessed of such an ungovernable bad temper and disposition as to deprive her of all reason and judgment."[3]

Several years after the divorce, due to mounting debts, bad business dealings, and people threatening his life because of his bad moral character, Moses claimed a man's right to a "fresh start", and with Minnie and Grace in tow, moved westward toward Minnesota. Moses bought a farm and settled down in Murray County sometime in 1874. He was not skilled at farming, so he took on other occupations, such as teacher, attorney, and justice of the peace.

CHAPTER TWO
The Rose Family

James Rose, son of Henry and Rebecca (Kent) Rose, was born in 1836 in Ohio. He was married to Martha Simons on November 6, 1858 in Pike County, Illinois by Reverend F. Snider.

James was a farmer, and times were tough for the newlyweds. So when he heard that volunteers were needed to fight for the cause, he enlisted as a private in Company C, 27th Infantry Regiment, Illinois on August 3, 1861. He said goodbye to his family and told them he'd be home soon.

After the battle of Belmont in November 1861, James marched about five miles and became overheated. He developed a severe cold, which settled in his head and caused his eardrums to rupture and discharge matter for over five months, impairing his hearing so that he was unable to hear ordinary conversation.

As a result of the injury, James Rose applied for an invalid pension, stating he was permanently disabled as a result of action in the war. He did receive a pension of $20 a month, which went toward farm expenses and raising a large family.

James and Martha had nine children: William, John, Cynthia (adopted), James N., Minnie, Clara Belle, Dora, Charlott, and Phillip. Cynthia was adopted when her mother died shortly after her birth while en route to California from Minnesota. The mother was Agnes Kent, a relative of Rebecca Kent.

There was much tragedy and misfortune in the Rose family. Shortly after the Civil War, when James and Martha lived in Fillmore County, they buried two children in Highland -- James N. and Minnie. Charlott, second youngest, died when she was just over a year old, and was buried in Tracy. And Dora suffered from ill health her entire life, committing suicide in April 1930.

CHAPTER THREE
William Rose

William Rose was the first born to James and Martha on January 9, 1860, in Perry, Illinois. From boyhood on, William was a reckless, devil-may-care sort of fellow. He loved notoriety and often, while straddling his buckskin pony, would ride across the prairie with a slouch hat and a buckskin suit, and declare himself a cowboy who was not afraid of man, devil, or beast. On one or two occasions, he was arraigned before minor officers of the law on petty offenses, and receiving a mild punishment, would openly declare vengeance on all who had a hand in his arrest.

But despite his reckless nature, Rose always helped his father with the daily chores, tended the livestock, and looked after his siblings. However, he was not fond of his neighbor, Moses Lufkin, who was known in those parts as an eccentric old man who lived with his two young daughters in Shetek Township. The daughters were bright and intelligent, but being deprived of a mother's care and training at a young age, their life was not as pleasant as that of the average country girl, and they seemed to shy away from strangers.

The Roses and the Lufkins had petty differences such as often arise between neighbors. From year to year the quarreling increased in bitterness until William Rose grew to manhood, when a new element entered into the difficulties between neighbors. William Rose sought to win the heart and hand of Grace, but Lufkin forbade William to show his attentions toward his daughter, and this sparked the bitter feud between the two families.

William Rose
(Courtesy of Redwood County Historical Society)

William Rose first met Moses Lufkin on October 19, 1874, at his father's house, the day they came from Fillmore County. The following winter, Rose went to school at Lufkin's house with John Averill, the nearby neighbor friend; his brother, John; Mary Robbins, and others. Lufkin was the teacher; his daughter, Minnie helped with the school activities, as did Mary Robbins.

One day, shortly after the daily school lessons, Lufkin and Minnie went into the west room of the home. Rose, age 15 at the time, opened the door between the east and west rooms and saw Lufkin with his hand under Minnie's clothes.

Rose exclaimed, "What are you doing?"

Lufkin replied, "It's none of your damned business."

Rose immediately slammed the door.

The next morning before school started, Lufkin was about to kiss Mary Robbins in Rose's presence, and he was appalled by this. Miss Robbins pushed Lufkin away and left the room.

At noon, Mary Robbins went toward the slough on her way home from school, and Lufkin followed her. Moses walked briskly to catch up to Mary, who stood near the slough watching the ducks swim around in the water.

He said, "Miss Robbins, please forgive me for my previous advances earlier today. I don't know what came over me."

"Don't you ever come near me again or I'll report your impropriety to the authorities," she said.

"You can be assured it won't happen again, Miss Robbins," replied Moses.

Later that day, Lufkin spoke to Rose about his advances toward Mary Robbins, and he denied being guilty of any impropriety.

Rose said, "You know you are a liar."

Lufkin picked up a ruler and threatened to whip Rose with it. After this, Rose always kept a keen eye on Lufkin, and steered clear of his advances and heated tirades.

While Rose attended school at the Lufkins, he became infatuated with Lufkin's daughter, Grace, the moment he set eyes on her. He spoke to her every day at school, and always managed to be with her in a private place every chance he got.

At first Grace wanted nothing to do with Rose, but as time went by, she fell in love with him. He treated her with kindness and respect – qualities she had not encountered while living with her domineering father.

Lufkin hated Rose and didn't like his attentions toward his young daughter. Whenever he saw the two together in a cozy conversation, Grace would be subject to her father's tirades and harsh words.

"Grace, I thought I told you to stay away from that good for nothin' Rose," shouted Lufkin. "He'll bring you nothin' but heartache. He's a womanizer and will not be true to you."

"And how do you know this?" asked Grace.

"Believe me, I know. Word gets around in a small town and I've heard plenty of stories about Will Rose, and his rovin' eye for the ladies," replied Lufkin. "Not only that; he's too old for you to be hangin' around with," cried Lufkin. "My goodness, you're nothin' but a child, Grace. What do you see in this boy?"

"But Father, I love Will and he loves me, and we plan to marry one day," said Grace.

"It'll be over my dead body," hollered Lufkin. "And I mean what I say. I don't want you seein' Will Rose no more. If you do, you'll suffer a good whippin' over my knee. And if that good for nothin' Rose shows attentions toward you again, and I find out about it, there'll be fists a-flyin'. Mark my words; I'm not foolin' around no more about the matter."

"But what shall I tell him, Father? He won't believe me when I say I don't wish to see him no more, and we are together every day in school."

Lufkin replied, "Never you mind; I'll have words with Rose after school tomorrow and make it damn clear, his attentions toward you are not to my likin'. And, Grace, I'm wantin' you to make it clear to the boy, I'm forbiddin' it, and he'll have me to deal with if I see him showin' attentions toward you again."

The following day after school, Lufkin pulled Rose aside and demanded he stop seeing his daughter.

Rose made it clear to Lufkin, "I'm in love with your daughter, wish to marry her one day, and will continue to see her, and there's not a damn thing you can do about it."

This remark sent Lufkin into a rage. Raising a fist, he hollered, "If I ever find out you're seeing Grace behind my back, I'll put a bullet in you, and that's for sure."

Rose said, "Don't you threaten me; you're nothin' but a lonely ol' man that don't want Grace to be happy."

"That's not true," replied Lufkin. "I just don't want to see her heart get broke, and I don't believe you'd be true to her, from the stories I've heard around town about you and the ladies."

Rose replied, "You don't know nothin' about me," and stormed out of the house. Grace heard the door slam hard, and ran outside after Rose. She finally caught up with him near the barn and said, "What did Father say to get you so upset?"

"He does not want me to show my attentions toward you, and we cannot see each other no more," replied Rose.

"I love you, Will, but maybe it's best we stop seeing each other, at least for a while."

"Grace, I still want us to be together one day," said Rose.

"Mark my words, we will be together, Will -- if not in this world, then in the next," cried Grace.

Grace was a rebellious young girl, and did not heed her father's warnings. She continued to see Rose on the sly, and they were together every chance they got. Grace would often sneak out of her bedroom window late at night after her father was asleep, to rendezvous with Rose at a secret spot near the slough, where they spent intimate time together. Rose promised Grace he'd marry her one day, and Grace believed him, for they were madly in love with each other. Their relationship grew into a budding romance despite Lufkin's constant meddling.

But after many months of sneaking around, Grace and Rose finally decided it best to end the affair in order to keep peace in the Lufkin household. It seems every time Lufkin found out that Grace and Rose had been together, Grace suffered the consequences of a whippin' from her ol' man.

CHAPTER FOUR
A Cow Gets Loose

One day, while Rose was out surveying the crops, he noticed Lufkin's cow in his cornfield again. He was tired of chasing Lufkin's old black-and-white cow out of the field, and was going to have words with him despite the hard feelings between them. He immediately saddled his pony and rode the few miles to Lufkin's to inform him that his cow had escaped again, and was wreaking havoc on the cornfield. This had to stop, or something quite severe would be levied on ol' man Lufkin.

As soon as Rose arrived at the Lufkin farm, he first looked for Moses in the barn, but didn't find him there. Instead, he found Grace huddled in a dark corner of the barn, sobbing uncontrollably. Rose rushed to her side and said, "Why are you crying, my dear?"

Grace replied, "My father's in bed with Minnie again doing terrible things, and I don't know how to stop him. He has such a violent temper; I'm afraid of him."

"Don't worry, Grace; I'll take care of it," replied Rose in a rage.

"No -- don't go in there; leave them be. You know my father despises you, doesn't want you near me or to set foot on his property," cried Grace.

"I'll deal with him. This has to stop. Your father knows it's wrong to be intimate with his daughter. Grace, you stay here, I'll confront your father about the matter."

Rose briskly walked to the house, softly climbed three wooden stairs, and opened the creaking screen door. He heard muffled voices coming from the bedroom and gently opened the door to find Lufkin on top of Minnie in intimate relations.

Rose cried, "What do you think you're doing? Get off her right now,

Lufkin! You know what you're doing is wrong. I've a mind to report this to the authorities."

Lufkin cried, "It's none of your damned business what I do in this house. This is my property and you're trespassin'. Get out of my house right now or I'll get the sheriff to pay you a visit."

Rose stormed out of the house and ran to the barn where Grace was waiting.

"What did you say to Father?" asked Grace.

"I told him I'm going to report his impropriety to the authorities."

"Oh, Will, I wish you wouldn't; it'll only make things worse for Minnie and me to live here, and we have nowhere else to go."

"Don't worry, Grace; I'll think of something. I best get out of here -- I've heard your ol' man keeps a loaded gun nearby, and he may have a mind to use it," exclaimed Rose.

By this time, Rose was so upset by the whole affair that he mounted his buckskin pony and left Lufkin's without ever mentioning the episode of the cow being loose in his cornfield.

The manner in which the knowledge of the incest came to Rose, both shocking and revolting, leaving enduring feelings of such disgust -- feelings so peculiar in themselves that they were hard to describe -- left a lasting and malicious impression on his young mind.

CHAPTER FIVE
Minnie Marries

At a young age, Minnie was given the task of keeping house, caring for her sister, Grace, and helping her father with school activities in their home. She was also forced to share her father's bed at times.

When Minnie was 15 years of age, there were rumors that she had been over to the neighbors and borrowed cash from Mr. Averill to purchase a gun so she could defend herself against her father. Minnie felt that if she threatened him with a gun, he would leave her alone, but the sight of a weapon did not deter Lufkin in the least, and he continued using Minnie as his wife.

Minnie was a very shy girl but easily made friends with the schoolchildren. She always had her eye on the handsome neighbor boy, Frank Foster, and they developed a special friendship. She finished her schooling at the age of 17 and moved to Winona to further her education, and escape the harsh demands of her father. But it was only a year later when she moved back to the farm to keep house for her father and look after Grace, who was 16 at the time. No one is sure why she moved home; it could have been she missed her sister, or her father demanded she return home to help with housekeeping and chores on the farm.

Shortly after Minnie returned home, she became bored with the routine of daily life on the farm and didn't have any plans for the future. She kept in close contact with Frank Foster while he was away at college in Chicago, and through their many letters, a long distance romance developed. In 1883 they were wed in Murray County. For the first time in her life, Minnie was happy. She had finally escaped her father's violent temper and manipulative ways, but poor Grace was alone once again.

Not everyone was happy for the newlyweds. It seems Frank's family never attended the wedding. Frank's father, Brigham, a religious, God-fearing man, absolutely despised Moses Lufkin and his evil ways, and never condoned the marriage.

Frank realized his father would never forgive him for marrying a Lufkin, so he and Minnie moved to Illinois, where he set up his law practice and became a very prominent attorney throughout South Chicago. They had three daughters: Libby, Nellie, and Amy.

Raising three small daughters, promoting his law practice, and being involved with community organizations and activities all put quite a strain on the marriage, along with some financial difficulties. Frank made lots of money, but was known to spend lots of it, too. At the end of every day, Frank recorded his earnings in a diary.

Minnie Lufkin Foster ca. 1900's
(Courtesy of Steven Foster, great nephew of Frank Foster)

Frank and Minnie quarreled often over money. It always seemed like there was never enough. Foster spent quite a bit of money on expensive suits in order to look his best during court proceedings. He invested in real estate and stocks, and, at one time, owned a very large passenger steamship that eventually went bankrupt.

Minnie became disheartened by Frank's spendthrift ways. Having been raised in a household where money was scarce and times were tough, Minnie never felt secure in the relationship.

Many years went by before Minnie finally tired of all the quarreling over money, moved out, and lived with her daughter, Libby, in Oklahoma. She never spoke to Frank again, and he died a pauper at the age of 59.[1]

CHAPTER SIX
Grace Meets Barney

Before Minnie married and moved out of the house, she gave Grace her small handgun. Minnie had purchased the gun years ago and threatened her father with it on several occasions. Now that she was married, she had no use for the weapon and passed it on to Grace. On days when Lufkin went to town, the sisters spent time at the slough shooting at a special target they made from scraps of wood found in the barn. Grace became an excellent sharpshooter.

After Minnie married, Grace was devastated, again left all alone with her evil father, who tried to get her to share his bed on numerous occasions.

Grace grew weary from quarreling with her father about this matter and one night confronted him. "I'll never share your bed, and stop insisting I do so. You know it's wrong to be intimate with me. I've put a lock on my bedroom door and I sleep with the loaded gun that Minnie gave me under my pillow. Don't you ever come near me, 'cause if you do, I'll pull the trigger, and don't think I'm scared to use it."

"Don't worry, Grace, I don't want no trouble. I'll never ask you to share my bed again, and that's a promise," replied Lufkin.

"You best make sure you don't, or I'll report your intentions to the authorities. I'm sure they'll believe me after I tell them what you did with Minnie for so many years," said Grace.

She never put much stock in her father's promise to her, as he was known to be quite the liar. From that day forward, before she went to bed each night, Grace made sure her door was locked and the gun tucked beneath her pillow.

Grace finished school at 18 and went on to become a teacher. Her first teaching position was in District 16, near her home, where she continued to keep house for her father. Living with her ol' man was not to her liking, as she despised him for putting an end to her romance with Rose, but what could she do; she had nowhere else to go.

Once Lufkin put an end to the love affair, Grace never saw much of Rose again. Years went by, and in the spring of 1884 Rose went to Campbell County, South Dakota and took up a homestead there. He remained on the homestead until the spring of 1887, when he returned to his Murray County home.

Grace went on with her life and tried to forget about Rose, but he always held a special place in her heart. She was lonely and wanted to move out of her father's house, but felt she would be there until the day she married. She didn't expect she'd ever get the chance to spend the rest of her life with Rose, as long as her ol' man was around.

In July 1886, Grace met Barney Benjamin at Sunday school and saw him each week at church or Bible class. Barney was 30 years of age, 6 feet in height, weighed about 180 pounds, and had a fair complexion, blue eyes, and light-brown hair. He had a peculiar contraction of the eyebrows. He was born in Hudson, Wisconsin, but had recently moved to Murray County and was working for C.P. Gould, a farmer, who lived one mile from the Lufkin home.

Barney first called upon Grace in August of that year and his conduct was always that of a gentleman. Their courtship was brief. Benjamin asked Moses for Grace's hand in marriage and on October 14, 1886, they were united in matrimony, with Moses Lufkin, Justice of the Peace, performing the ceremony at the home of Wesley Averill, a nearby neighbor and friend.

Grace looked forward to the first night with her husband, but the long-awaited honeymoon turned into a fiendish nightmare. Grace describes her wedding night best:

We were married about 7 o'clock in the evening. I had never been married before; was a virgin at that time. On the marriage night, one minute after we were in bed, he threw up my nightgown, pulled my knees apart, and I felt something running over me. He did not speak to me that night fondly or caress me in any manner. His actions and demeanor were altogether different than before marriage. His private parts appeared to me, to be not as nature intended.

We lived and cohabited together eight days in my father's house once married, and each night I slept with my husband, he never treated me kindly, all he seemed to care for was to indulge in his passions. By the eighth night, he wanted to cohabit with me further, but I refused because I could not endure it any longer for the reason of the unsavory way he treated me; there was no pleasure for me in intimacy.[1]

Late that night, Grace finally confided in her father about the way Barney was treating her. Around midnight, ol' man Lufkin forced Barney from the home at gunpoint. Lufkin threatened to shoot him if he ever saw him again. Barney immediately left the area and never returned.

After Barney deserted Grace, she started investigating his background to find out what sort of a man she had married. She first wrote a letter to the postmaster in Hudson, Wisconsin, where Barney said he lived all his life, but was informed by them that no person by that name had ever been heard of there.

Next, she learned that his name was not Barney Benjamin, but Christian Nelson; he'd been convicted previously of the crime of forgery and served a year in the Meeker County Jail. He had committed several other forgeries around the same time as the one for which he was imprisoned.

Neighbors informed Grace of Barney's true character: that of a corrupt and immoral man. He was not the religious, upstanding gentleman he portrayed himself to be during their brief courtship. People said he consorted with women of bad repute, especially a Mrs. Campbell, a known prostitute, and it was by reason of his relations with this woman that he had been led into the crime of forgery that caused his arrest. There were rumors that Barney already had a wife when he married Grace.

In December 1886, Grace met with attorney F.S. Brown of Tracy to file for an annulment of her marriage on "the grounds that defendant's name was not Barney Benjamin, but Chris Nelson, a convicted felon, and an immoral and depraved man, and that at the time he was married to plaintiff, he had another wife then living. And on further grounds, that at the time of the marriage, defendant was, from sickness or other cause, incapable of consummating marriage ..."[2]

The Summons and Complaint was personally served on Barney Benjamin on December 17, 1886 in Pipestone by Sheriff Edgar Shephard. Barney did not appear in court and nobody could locate his whereabouts to finalize the legal proceedings. It was rumored he fled to Dakota Territory, but no one knew a definite location.

It wasn't until May 1887 that Judge A.D. Perkins finally granted Grace an annulment of her marriage. Grace continued to live with her father after the annulment.

CHAPTER SEVEN
Fire Bombing

One late night in June 1887, while the Lufkins were asleep, an explosion was heard at the rear of the house. The bomb consisted of a can of powder with chunks of railroad iron bound around it with wire. No one was injured in the blast.

Grace was quite sure she recognized the voice of Will Rose calling to someone and running away immediately after the explosion.

The following morning, the Lufkins found several torches composed of strips of calico and other cloth soaked in kerosene that had been fired and placed against their house at the same time, and a jug containing kerosene that had been thrown through the window and broken, saturating the kitchen floor with kerosene to make the work of the fire surer, but the fire never ignited properly, and burned itself out before it did any damage.

Lufkin stoutly maintained that the Roses (William and John) were the instigators of the plot, but William Rose wasn't arrested for this incident until February 1888, some seven months after the fact.

The evidence against Rose for arson was of such a slim character that a conviction was out of the question, and the case was immediately dismissed by the Grand Jury in April 1888.

There were many people who believed that Lufkin had done the work himself in order to create sympathy, and to get rid of his troublesome neighbors by having them locked up in jail for arson. Proof of this was a copy of *The Chicago InterOcean* newspaper found on a stake near a fence on Lufkin's property. This newspaper, published in Chicago from 1865 to 1907, appealed to an upscale readership. With the expansion of the railway system, it was possible to deliver weekly newspapers to business people across America. Moses Lufkin could have received an issue of this newspaper from his daughter, Minnie, who lived in Chicago at the time. It was very unlikely that Rose would acquire an upscale newspaper such as this.

CHAPTER EIGHT
Incest Trial

James Rose came before W.S. Root, Justice of the Peace, and filed a criminal complaint in February 1888, stating that Moses Lufkin committed the crime of incest upon the body of Alice B. Sloan at the town of Shetek, Murray County, on the 25th day of March 1887.

The following is a portion of witness testimony in Moses Lufkin's incest trial, and gives an intimate look into the lives of the characters in this story.

A portion of James Rose's testimony follows:

My son, John, and his wife started from home that day to go up to Lufkin's house. I went a little afterward. We all got to Lufkin's about together. I passed John and his wife on the road east of Lufkin's house. I was riding a gray mare. John and his wife went to Lufkin's door before I did. The door was on the south side of the house. John's wife skipped out when she looked in at the door. John motioned to me with his finger. John was standing just at the left-hand side of Lufkin's door and partly in the doorway. The storm door was open and the inner door shoved open. I went to the door and took a look. I saw the face of Alice B. Sloan; she had her face turned a little to the right from Lufkin. She was lying on her back with her legs spread and the defendant was lying between her legs. Lufkin had his pants and coat on. I saw Lufkin there and then having connection with Alice B. Sloan, the same as man and wife. She had on a pair of white drawers. After I saw this I went and unhitched my mare and rode over to a stack of hay. I was not over 7

or 8 feet from Lufkin and Alice B. Sloan when they were lying on
the bed without any covering. I do not know who Alice B. Sloan is.

"Do you know what the common report in this community is as to
her identity?" asked the attorney.

"I do, the common report is that Alice B. Sloan is the niece of
Moses Lufkin, the daughter of his sister," replied James.

"Have you ever heard defendant admit or state that Alice B. Sloan
was his niece?"

James Rose replied, "I have; at one time at Lufkin's house I wanted
some writing copied and Moses said, 'You had better have my niece,
Alice, copy it off.' Alice B. Sloan was standing right by...."[1]

John Rose's testimony was similar to his father's:

Myself, wife and father were going to Lufkin's residence; my wife
and I starting a little before father. The storm door was open. The
inner door was not latched. I shoved door open, wife was with me,
and we both could see what was going on in the bed and who was
on the bed.

My wife says: "This is no place for me." She ran along the south side
of the house, passing to the north of the trees. Did not see her again
until she was nearly home.

On the bed lay Lufkin and Alice B. Sloan, she on her back with
her legs opened and defendant between them, going through the
motion that men do when they have connection with a woman.
This took place in Lufkin's house in Shetek Township, Murray
County, Minnesota on or about March 25th, 1887.

"Do you know what the common report in the vicinity in which she lives in as to her identity?" asked the attorney.

"I do. The common report is that Alice B. Sloan is the niece of defendant, the daughter of his sister," replied John Rose.₂

Moses Lufkin testified on his own behalf, and part of his statement follows:

I have lived in Shetek for 13 years and am defendant in this action. I know Alice B. Sloan. She came to reside with me February 27th, 1887 at 3:00 pm. At that time she was full of disease. She was not very sick when she first came there. She was rheumatic and had cramps but it was three weeks before I found she was very bad.

On the 23rd, 24th, 25th, and 26th of March, Alice Sloan was confined to her bed, and had been several days prior. The doctor told me not to let her get up from bed. The outside door on south side of house near west side was composed of inner door and storm door. Those doors were blocked up and not used during the winter. March 23rd through the 26th, the doors were fastened by locking, to prevent parties from coming in on Alice while sick. The storm door was fastened on outside by a latch. The inner door was fastened on inside by turning lock. These doors were both kept locked during March 23rd through 26th and the outer door kept latched.

The testimony of James and John Rose relative to my conduct with Alice was untrue. They lied. Neither John or James Rose or John's wife were at my place about March 25th.

When Moses was asked, "What relation is Alice B. Sloan to you?"

Moses replied, "I don't know who Alice B. Sloan is. She is a stranger to me up to November 1886. I don't know if she was a relative or not. When Alice first came to my house, I did not know she was sick at all."[3]

Grace Lufkin was a witness for her father and part of her testimony follows:

I am the defendant's daughter. I know Alice Sloan and keep house for father. When Alice came there I thought she was well but tired. Soon after, she complained of cramps and rheumatism. Ever since she came there, I have had charge of her, assisted by father. I was home all the time March 23rd through 26th, 1887. I was home all the time except one day, Alice and I went up to Fulda in the first part of March.

John Rose was not at my house about March 25th, nor James Rose nor John's wife. The testimony of John Rose that I heard is false. Alice and I slept together and father upstairs.[4]

Hiram Lakin, nephew of Lufkin, testified as follows:

I teach school; have taught 20 terms of 4 months average. I know the defendant. Know James and John Rose. Know Alice Sloan since March 24th, 1887. Saw her there at Lufkin's house in Murray County. That was the first time I ever saw her. I went to Lufkin's house about 9 o'clock that morning. I remained there until dusk. Alice was sick. She was lying on the bed. Only one room in the house was occupied; the one which has been described. The reason I know it was March 24th is because Lufkin had borrowed money from me and I had to give him ten days notice and I gave him notice that day. I was there the 25th all day. Did not see James, John or

Mrs. Rose there. Lufkin was not there when I went there on the 25th. He came about a few minutes before 2:00 pm. We sat down to discuss things at 2:00 pm. I left Lufkin's on the evening of the 24th. Returned the next morning and left again that evening. Did not see any of the Roses at Lufkin's. While I was there, no such occurrence occurred between Lufkin and Alice as was detailed by the prosecution. I was in that room all the time I was in the house. I returned to Lufkin's Monday evening, March 28 and stayed there until Thursday morning. Did not see any of the Roses.[5]

The Grand Jury thoroughly investigated this case, failed to find an indictment, and the charges were dismissed against Moses Lufkin on April 20, 1888. The jury stated they believed Alice Sloan to be an innocent and virtuous girl.[6]

CHAPTER NINE
Slander Cases

A short time after James Rose filed a formal complaint against Lufkin for incest on Alice B. Sloan, Lufkin turned around and filed four separate slander suits against his neighbors, Wesley and Rossanah Averill, and James and Martha Rose.

V.B. Seward was the attorney for the defendants in each and every slander case. Seward studied law at Mankato under M.G. Willard and at Stillwater under Congressman J.N. Castle. He was admitted to the bar in September 1878, practiced in Mankato until the spring of 1879, and then took up his residence in Marshall. He served as County Attorney of Lyon County four terms and was elected state senator from the Seventeenth District in 1906, serving one term. Mr. Seward was an exceptional attorney and a leading citizen of his community.

Wesley Averill was set to testify in April 1888, but was unable to appear at court by reason of a fracture of one of his ribs, according to the affidavit submitted by C.L. Bohauman, M.D.

Averill was the defendant in this action and an important material witness. Lufkin was aware that Averill had accidentally injured his rib, but it was not until the evening of the 16th day of April that he was aware of its serious nature, and up to that time believed that Averill would be able to appear and testify in the said actions.

The following are partial witness depositions taken from court documents in April 1888.

Averill would have testified as follows if sworn as a witness in this action:

It was sometime in April 1874 at St. Charles in Winona County that I saw Moses Lufkin and his daughter in bed together and that neither Moses nor his daughter, Minnie, had any clothing on save their ordinary night clothes. And that Minnie was, at that time, of the age of fourteen years and over.

Averill would further testify that on the 13th day of May 1875 at Shetek in Murray County:

Minnie Lufkin came to me and asked me to loan her the sum of five dollars and that the reason she made such request was that she wished the money to buy a revolver with which to defend herself against her father. Moses Lufkin had used her as his wife several times, and was still trying to use her as his wife. I loaned Minnie the five dollars. Averill further states, on the 15th day of June 1876 in Shetek, I saw the plaintiff and his daughter, Minnie, in bed together undressed.[1]

George Lufkin, nephew of Moses Lufkin, gave his statement before R. Edson Doolittle, a Notary Public in Eau Claire, Wisconsin. A portion of his deposition follows:

I knew Moses Lufkin for about twenty years, while he resided at Phillips in Franklin County, Maine from 1853 to about 1873. I lived in his house for about one year with my mother. The first talk I ever heard about him was when I was about four years old, and I continued to hear talk about his bad character all the time until he left. His reputation for chastity and decency was bad during all that time.

When I was about six years old, I remember he came to our house and was sick with a sore throat and it was reputed there at the time that he had what they called syphilis and people seemed to think it was disgraceful and that he was a bad man.

In the fall of 1866, when I was seventeen years old, and while we were living at Lufkin's house, they were having revival meetings at the schoolhouse, and he took an active part in those meetings, and one evening he came home from one of these meetings, and brought with him a young woman by the name of Electra Record, and said she was under concern of mind and that he must be with her all the time and not be interrupted until he got her converted. He stayed with her every night for a week in a bedroom where there was only one bed, and nearly all the time in the day time, during that time.

One day he told us that he wanted to tell Electra that the house was vacant, and told us that we must move out at once. We moved within a few days and as soon as we had moved away, this woman, Electra Record, went back to his house and kept house for him five or six months.

From this time until about the year 1873, when he finally left that place, he had the general reputation of keeping as housekeepers women of bad repute. I remember some of the names of these women, one by the name of Elizabeth Bowley, Elvira Lufkin and Hannah Morse. He had the reputation of running around with other lewd women and staying with them nights at various places and it was currently reported that he did so. It was currently reported in that neighborhood and believed by the people in general that he was threatened with mob violence and that he left that place on account of these threats rather than give up his bad practices.[2]

SLANDER CASES

Emma Manchester, sister to George Lufkin, gave her statement:

In the fall of 1867, Moses came to our house and asked my mother, in my presence, to let me grant housekeeping for him. He said he wanted to reform and get a better reputation, and he said he thought he could be better able to reform, if my mother would let me go and keep house for him, and he said that as I was his niece, the people would not be so apt to talk about him if I went, as they would, if he got someone who was not a relative.

Mother finally consented to let me go and I went in October of that year to keep house for him. When I had been there a short time, he went to the depot to meet a young, widow woman by the name of Hannah Morse and brought her home with him. She was his cousin and seemed to us at the time, to be a respectable woman. She stayed there till sometime in the latter part of February most of the time.

Lufkin and this woman sat up nights a good deal, and were out nights a good deal. He told me that he was going to marry her. He had one cow that gave milk, and he milked the cow till some time after she came, and then she would go out and they said she went to milk the cow, because he had a stiff finger which bothered him in milking. All the time when she went to the barn to milk, he went with her, and they generally stayed a long time, and many times for an hour or more, and as an excuse for these things, he told me he was going to marry her. About two weeks after this, Hannah Morse went away in February 1868.

I woke up one night and Lufkin was getting into my bed. I stopped him, and he sat down on the edge of the bed and told me that if I would do as he wanted me to, that I might have a good home as long as I wanted it, and that he would buy me nice clothes, and that it would be better for my health, if I would let him sleep with me.

I would not consent to let him in, and then he said he would get in anyway, whether I wanted him to or not, and he took hold of me and tried to force me to let him into bed. Then I told him if he did not let me be and go out, I would start screaming and raise the neighbors. He seemed to be afraid I would then and went out.

Then I got up and put my trunk and what things I could, that were in the room, and put them against my door, as there was no lock on it, and stayed there until morning. In the morning I told him I was going home and he told me I better stay and he would get a lock and put it on the door and I could lock it every night, but I went home and did not go back again.[3]

Loretta Gray, an acquaintance of Lufkin, provided her statement as follows:

I have been acquainted with Moses Lufkin for about twenty years, when he resided in Franklin County, Maine up to 1873. His reputation for chastity and decency was bad.

About the first that I heard about him was that he was too intimate with his sister who kept house for him. This sister is the mother of the girl who now keeps house for him.

I was about eight years old at the time, and Lufkin's sister, who then lived with him, used to come to where I lived, about a mile away, and get me to go over and stay with her. I stayed with her a good many nights. He was always away when I went home with her, and I remember once Moses said, 'Have you brought that little brat with you again?'

I remember once a Mrs. Reed, one of our neighbors, called me into her house, and after giving me some little presents, asked me if I knew that Lufkin and his sister slept together, and I was asked this same thing by several other neighbors. They all seemed to think that Lufkin and his sister did sleep together.

When she came after me, for the first few weeks, I did not want to go with her, and she seemed to be afraid to be alone with Lufkin, her brother, and she would often cry and tease me until I would go with her. She gave me several presents to get me to go and stay with her. She was then about sixteen years old. After several weeks, she stopped asking me to come there and stay with her, but she remained there.

I remember after this, and before he left Franklin County, Maine, he was taken sick and came to our house, and the family and neighbors talked about there being sores on his body, and they all seemed to think he had been doing something he ought not to do. I did not then understand what was the trouble with him, but his throat was sore, and I understood afterwards, and it was generally understood and talked about, that he had some venereal disease.

After this and in the same town and neighborhood, he was married and then he and his wife were divorced, and then during the last seven or eight years he lived in that county and up to about 1873, he had several different housekeepers, some of whom were notoriously bad characters, and all had bad reputations.

The reputation of his house became so bad that it was shunned by all respectable persons, and Lufkin was threatened with mob violence. One evening I remember, he was walking home from church with one of these women, and he was followed by a lot of boys and young men who threw sticks at him and threatened him with further violence if he did not change his way of living. I heard this last from the neighbor and it was reputed to be true by the people generally in that neighborhood.

There was so much talk against him and so much threatening, that it was understood, when he left the neighborhood, that he was afraid to remain longer, for fear of being attacked by mobs for his bad practices.[4]

Flora Woodruff, niece of Moses Lufkin, gave her statement:

I live in Minneapolis. In 1874, I lived a mile and a half north of Dover Center, Olmstead County. My uncle, Moses Lufkin, came to visit me for the first time in the afternoon and we visited very pleasantly until bed time.

My husband being an invalid, I took the lamp to light my uncle's way to his bed. I passed up the stairs and into the room ahead of my uncle, walked to the head of the bed and set the lamp down on the stand. I turned to go back, and as I turned, it brought me face to face with my uncle. He clasped me tight in his arms, drew me tight to him and said, 'I wish you would lay with me tonight.' I tore myself away from him and went down the stairs. This happened in the spring of 1874. He had come recently from the east and came to make me a visit.

I know nothing since of Mr. Lufkin's family. I have always heard from our relatives that his character was disreputable. I have heard this same story from several parties. I certainly know his reputation. I have never heard anything as to his business reputation, only as to his moral character, and I will swear that his reputation is bad.[5]

Lufkin's slander suits were never heard in court, as his death preceded this action.

CHAPTER TEN
Shot in the Back

By 1888, the feud between the Lufkins and the Roses had escalated, and both parties were on edge awaiting the court date for the upcoming slander suit. Moses was in fear of his life with the constant threats from the Rose family, whose farm site was adjacent to his. Lufkin felt he was being watched and followed by members of the Rose family, as it seemed he'd run into them everywhere he went. Moses seldom ventured out of his home during the day. The nights were long and tedious after Grace left. At some point, Grace had moved to Iowa for a teaching position. A couple years later, she moved in with her sister in Chicago.

As a way to improve his situation, Lufkin decided to sell his farm, and move in with his niece, Fannie Slover, who lived nearby. He felt this decision would improve his lot considerably -- he would have the money needed to pay his legal fees for the upcoming slander suit, and he'd avoid any further confrontations with the Rose family.

Sometime in May of that year, Lufkin moved in with the Slovers, who resided in the Town of Gales, Redwood County, Minnesota. Lufkin was comfortable with the arrangements and assured the Slovers that this was a temporary situation and he'd leave as soon as the slander suit was settled.

Slover's house was quite comfortable. It contained a room measuring 16' x 14' with one window to the east, one to the north, and one to the south. The north window was in the middle of the room. The lower sash of this window was partly raised, and on the outside of the window, fastened to the window casing, was mosquito netting.

In front of the window was a lounge, 5 feet 11 inches long, on which

Moses Lufkin enjoyed reclining, and this was his favorite resting place where he often sat in the evenings. By sitting in this location, his left shoulder rested against the window casing, leaving a portion of his back exposed to the window.

On a summer night in 1888, the Slovers settled in the sitting room after a fine supper of beef stew, cornbread, and homemade apple pie, all prepared by Fannie. The table was cleared and dishes were done by Eli's three daughters, and everyone seemed in good spirits.

It was a hot, brightly moonlit night, and Lufkin was enjoying a quiet evening of conversation in the sitting room with Eli, Fannie and two of their daughters. Lufkin was seated on the lounge by the open window, where a slight breeze cooled his sweating brow.

At about 8 o'clock on this evening of August 22, 1888, a bright light was burning from a kerosene lamp sitting on a table in the middle of the room. Near the east window sat Eli, looking at the light and conversing with Lufkin. In the northeast corner of the room sat one daughter, and near the table sat another daughter. On the west side of the room, Fannie was stooping over and sprinkling clothes, getting ready to iron.

Suddenly the group was startled by a loud noise and Lufkin fell over, shot through the back. As he fell he said, "Help, quick, I am shot through the body deader than hay."[1] Lufkin died about ten minutes later.

Slover jumped to the window and looked out. His little daughter said, "Father, do not go to the window, they will shoot you."

Slover replied, "No they won't, they have got their man, they won't hurt me."[2]

Slover looked out the window into the moonlit night. The yard to the north had some shrubbery in it. Farther to the north, a long line of tall willows obstructed the view. Slover said that he thought he saw a man about 25 feet away, between the window and the hedge, running. The man's back was to the window; his face and hands could not be seen. He did not see any gun or recognize any clothing that would identify the person fleeing. He did not declare to the family, at that time, who he

37

thought the person was, nor did he have anything more than a glance at a portion of the retreating figure.

Slover seized a gun hanging on the wall, rushed out the door on the south side of the house, looked around, and was unable to see anybody.

About one hour after the murder, Mr. Gales, a neighbor; Slover's son, Arthur; and another person drove to Tracy, about one mile north from the home of James Rose.

They notified the police officers at the time that Moses Lufkin had been shot and to shadow James Rose's house. This was merely speculation at this point, given the fact that the entire community knew of the feud and hatred between the Lufkins and the Roses.

Early the following morning on the 23rd, the police officers proceeded to James Rose's house and examined the condition of a buckskin pony picketed out near the house. They saw William Rose at the window looking out, but made no effort to arrest him.[3]

These facts are important in demonstrating that the arrest of Rose was not due to any identification of him by Eli Slover at the time, but was an afterthought when circumstances, and the discovery of pony tracks one mile east of Slover's house, thought suspicious, had been later ascertained.

Moses Lufkin, age 45
(Courtesy Steven Foster)

CHAPTER ELEVEN

The Arrest

The night of the shooting, it was impossible for Slover to identify the person fleeing from the window as William Rose. The discovery of a man's tracks in Slover's garden, the tracks of a horse one mile east of Slover's, at a place where a horse had been plainly tied in a tree-claim -- all this was discovered on the morning of August 23.

Not until after these tracks had been discovered and traced, and not until after it had been discovered that on the afternoon of August 22, an unknown man had been seen riding a buckskin pony in the vicinity where the tracks were found, northeast of Slover's house -- it was not until then that William Rose was mentioned as the man identified fleeing from the window.

On the morning of August 24, William Rose walked the short distance to Levi Montgomery's farm. Early that morning, after breakfast, the two men went out to the field to do some "stacking."

After stacking for several hours, they took a much-needed rest. Mr. Montgomery looked off into the distance and noticed a team coming from the southwest corner of the field.

"Who's that?" said Montgomery.

"Well, I don't know," said Rose.

As the team got closer, Montgomery said, "Oh, that's Mr. Craig and Mr. Segar."

Rose was resting on the ground, after the first load, with his hands folded up over his knees.

"Good morning, gentlemen," said Rose.

When the team finally came to a complete stop, Craig jumped off, pulled a revolver out of his pocket, pointed it toward Rose, and said, "Throw up your hands."

Rose didn't make any move at all, kind of laughed at him and said, "What's the matter with you folks anyway?"

Segar shouted in a loud voice, "Throw up your hands." Both men were apparently excited. Segar got out of the wagon, came over to where Rose was sitting, and said, "I believe we want you."

"Is that so?" said Rose.

"Yes," said Segar. "Now get up here so I can search you."

"Well, what's this all about? Why am I being searched?"

"Haven't you heard? Lufkin's been murdered, and you're a likely suspect," said Craig.[1]

Rose got up from the ground, Segar searched him, and irons were placed upon his wrists. "Now get in the wagon," hollered Segar.

Rose looked at Montgomery with bewilderment and said, "Tell my folks what's happened and have them meet me in New Ulm right away."

"Don't worry, Will, I'll take care of it; we'll be there as soon as we can," replied Montgomery.

Rose slowly walked to the wagon and climbed in, followed by Craig and Segar. The team immediately headed for New Ulm.

When they arrived at the jail in New Ulm, paperwork was completed and Sheriff Schmid placed Rose in a cell. It wasn't long before James and Martha Rose, and Levi Montgomery arrived. They asked the sheriff why their son had been arrested. The sheriff explained he'd been issued a "Warrant of Arrest" by Justice Joseph Libby, to take William Rose into custody on suspicion of the murder of Moses Lufkin, and he would be held at the Brown County Jail as there was no sufficient jail in Redwood County. Since the charge was not a bailable offense, Rose would remain in jail until the formal examination scheduled in Lamberton in a few days.

James and Martha Rose had tears in their eyes as they hugged their son and said their goodbyes. They left the jail with heavy hearts, knowing their son did not commit the crime, but hoping he'd be home soon.

At the time of his arrest, Rose had on a wide-brimmed hat, a check-ered-colored coat, blue overalls, and a pair of plow shoes.

CHAPTER TWELVE

Coroner's Inquest

The formal coroner's inquest for the death of Moses Lufkin was held at Lamberton on August 30, 1888 before Justice of the Peace, Joseph E. Libby, and lasted two days.

At the inquest, Michael M. Madigan was the prosecuting attorney, and F.S. Brown of Tracy appeared on behalf of William Rose. There were about 30 witnesses examined.

Dr. Pease examined Lufkin's body after the shooting on August 23, and gave a report of his findings at the inquest:

From the size of the ball, the weapon used was at least .44 caliber. The ball entered through the back of the body of the deceased at a point 3 1/4 inches to the right of the spinal column and passed in a horizontal line through the body, 6 inches below a transverse line between the nipples and 4 inches above the navel. The wound was only examined externally. The wound in front of the body was not as clean cut as in the back, and the lips of the wound were inverted in the back, while the wound in front, the lips were turned out, and with more lacerations around the wound. I also discovered the holes through the clothing, and examined the body for other marks of injury, by pulling the pantaloons about the ankles; and the upper garments, pulled them up to the neck and shoulders, not removing them. Lufkin had on a jacket and what we call a "mackinaw" shirt. His outer clothing, I think, was what is called "overall goods." The wound entered the body almost horizontally, and was considered to be a mortal wound. He died within 10 minutes. No post-mortem examination was done of this man.[1]

Slover gave a statement of the details of the crime and said he saw a person fleeing from the outside of the window right after the shooting that night.

When asked by the attorney, "Who would you say that person was?"

Slover replied, "In my opinion, I would say it was William Rose."[2]

Slover described where the bullet entered the screen, that the muzzle had been held so close to the window that the mosquito bar on the outside was singed where the shot had gone through, and how he found a mark on the oil stove where the bullet had struck it and landed on the floor.

He further stated, "I do not know whether the deceased had any money or not. I have not searched the deceased or his trunk since the shot was fired. I do not know whether the deceased made a 'will' prior to his death, but I think he has -- he never told me so. I do not know who the beneficiaries are in the 'will.' I do not think the deceased's life was insured, but I think not. I did not examine the wound after the shot."

Slover admitted having three old Army muskets in the house -- one was loaded and the other two were not loaded. Slover stated that "Lufkin owned a revolver and always carried it with him, but did not know where that revolver was at this time."[3]

Some points brought out at the inquest were that Rose had been at Slover's house the Saturday before the homicide, claiming that he was over in that part of the country seeing parties living in the vicinity.

As he had no particular business at Slover's and was not on speaking terms with Lufkin, it was presumed he was looking over the grounds to acquaint himself with the premises in order to accomplish the murderous caper on another occasion.

On the afternoon of the homicide, several parties testified that they saw a man on a cream-colored pony, resembling Rose's, riding north in the direction of Slover's. Rose's hired man, Fred Schultz, testified that Rose left home on the afternoon of the murder and that he did not see him again until the following morning.

No attempt was made by Rose to prove an alibi or set up any defense at this time.

These were the main points of evidence. A verdict was rendered by the jury that the deceased was killed by William Rose. The evidence on which the verdict was based was entirely circumstantial, but Rose was held to answer the charge of murder at the next term of the district court, and was committed to the Brown County Jail in New Ulm, where he would spend the next three years of his life.[4]

While in jail, Rose became acquainted with Clifton Holden, who was placed in the jail on November 26, 1888 for murdering his cousin, Frank Dodge. Both men were found guilty on circumstantial evidence, and parts of both trials were conducted over the same period of time. Holden and Rose were often handcuffed together and shuffled between Brown County Jail and the Redwood County Courthouse. At the eleventh hour, Holden's sentence was commuted and he was transferred in May 1891 to Stillwater State Prison, where he served his life sentence.

It's been said that while Rose was incarcerated in the Brown County Jail, he developed a romantic relationship with a young German girl who was in jail for some petty offense. Her name was Alma, and she was only 16 years of age at the time. Alma became so infatuated with Rose that there was quite a scene one night before Rose was brought to Redwood Falls. She begged and pleaded with the sheriff to be allowed to see him, and Rose added his own entreating, but to no avail. They were not allowed to meet, and little Alma never got to say goodbye to William, her first love.[5]

Rose was bound over to the Grand Jury and in November 1888, he was indicted for the murder of Moses Lufkin. The case was tried at that term of court in Redwood County before Judge Webber. After hearing the case, the jury deliberated over four days. There was a disagreement of eight to four in favor of the defendant. Rose was acquitted.

At the next term of court in Redwood County in May 1889, Rose was again tried before Judge Webber. The trial lasted over two weeks and again the jury was unable to agree; seven to five in favor of the defendant. Rose was once again acquitted. Attorneys W.W. Erwin and F.S. Brown defended Rose on the two mistrials.

At each of these trials, Eli Slover testified that as soon as the shot was fired, he rushed to the window and saw whom he believed to be, Rose, disappearing in the distance. However, he was not positive of it, and at each of these trials, the jury was more in favor of acquittal than conviction.

At the next term in November 1889, Rose was tried a third time before Judge Webber.

CHAPTER THIRTEEN
The Third Trial

The third trial of William Rose was held in Dunnington Hall at the Redwood County Courthouse on November 12, 1889. At this trial, Assistant Attorney General Childs made his plea to the jury in the Rose case, followed by Attorney Erwin for the defense.

The streets around the hall where court was in session were packed long before the opening of the court, and it was not hard to discern that the audience had no sympathy for Rose.[1]

The jury at the third trial was probably the most impartial and intelligent of any ever gathered on an important case in this section of the country. Its members were from all over Redwood County, with 12 men representing as many different towns. The jury had the distinguished honor of redeeming the good name of Redwood County, where it had been sarcastically said that no murderer could be convicted.

Assistant Attorney General Childs was to be commended for his success and the labor he put into the case. He had tried the case twice before, with disagreeing juries, but in this trial, he left no stone unturned. Slover spent most of the day at Attorney Madigan's office the day before the trial, getting prepared for his testimony, and was told to keep cool and calm.

The defense -- conducted by the greatest criminal lawyer of the state, William Erwin, and assisted by Judge Brown of Tracy -- had little to stand on, and not much of an alibi for Rose, but Attorney Erwin made a special effort, resulting in a plea that was long remembered by the people of that town.[2]

Several important points were brought out by the defense during the cross-examination of Eli Slover. The following is from court documents:

The first was the question asked by Erwin; "Do you know what became of Lufkin's will?" Erwin wanted to show that just before Lufkin died, he had a will, in possession of his associate, Judge Brown, that he took over to Slover's house a few days before the homicide, and now it had disappeared.

The prosecution objected to this as immaterial and irrelevant. At the inquest, Slover denied knowing anything about Lufkin's will.

Erwin asked Slover what he meant by the comment he made to his daughter the night of the shooting: "No they won't, they've got their man, they won't shoot me."

Slover stated, "Lufkin had repeatedly told me that William Rose would shoot him."

"Then when you went to the window, you thought of William Rose?" asked Erwin.

"Yes sir," replied Slover.

"You stated that you went outside after you heard the shot, and found that the dogs appeared frightened. How did they look afraid and what did they do?"

"They ran up to me and scrounged down. One was a little bull dog, and another a shepherd dog."

"Don't you know, sir, that if somebody fired a shot that the dogs knew, they would scrounge down, but if somebody that they didn't know fired it, they would bark to sound the alarm and protect their home."

"No, sir, I don't know any such thing." [3]

Other interesting points brought out by defense Attorney Erwin were that:

After the shooting, Slover sent his wife and youngest daughter, Clara to get help from the neighbors. He sent them to Mr. Croft's place a half mile away, rather than to their nearest neighbor, Mr. Grundin, who only lived 80 rods away. Mr. Croft lived twice as far away as Mr. Grundin. Slover stated that they were on friendly terms with Mr. Grundin, but instructed his wife to travel to Croft's place.

Since the previous trial, Slover gave conflicting testimony about where his three daughters were and what they were doing at the time of the shooting. Slover claimed, Angie, the eldest daughter, was in the bedroom that had a window in it on the south side of the house, and was not present when the shot was fired.

Erwin proved by demonstration that it was physically impossible for Slover to put his face up to the window immediately after Lufkin was shot as the lounge and Lufkin blocked the path to the window.

Erwin questioned several witnesses about pony tracks. These witnesses testified that pony tracks found near the Slover residence the morning after the homicide were made from a pony not shod, while the defendant's pony was shod in the front.

Charles Anderson, a blacksmith in the town of Tracy, testified for the defense.

"During the spring or summer of 1888, did the defendant bring a buckskin pony to your shop to be shod," asked Erwin.

"Yes."

"Who shod that pony?"

"I did."

"How did you shoe him?"

"I forget -- the way I shoed the rest of them."

"On the fore feet?"

"Yes sir."

"On the hind feet."

"No sir."[4]

James Rose was asked by Erwin, "Do you know when the shoes were taken off your son's buckskin pony?"

"Yes sir."

"When was it in 1888 when the shoes were taken off?"

"It was the 24th of August; the day my son was arrested."

"Who was there when the shoes were taken off?"

"Frank Simmons was in the stable at the time. There was a loose shoe there, and I guessed it would be well to take it off, and I took the shoes off, and Mr. Simmons held the pony's head."₅

Martha Rose, defendant's mother, stated that her son wore "gaiter shoes" when he left the house on the afternoon of August 22. At the request of the counsel, the defendant came forward for the purpose of allowing the witness to look at the shoes he had on. Martha verified they were the shoes he had on when he left the house that day. The plow shoes, offered into evidence by the State, and the shoes on the feet of the defendant, were compared by placing them together.

Erwin asked Martha Rose, "Have you ever worn those plow shoes?"

"I have worn them a great many times."

"Do you know who had them on the evening of the 22nd and the morning of the 23rd?"

"I do, I had them on myself."

"How did you come to have them on?"

"I put them on to do my milking and feed my calves and do my outdoor work."

"What time in the evening did you do your milking?"

"Somewhere between 7 and 8 o'clock; I had no regular time to milk."

"Did anyone come to your house on the afternoon of the 22nd?"

"Yes, Mary Potter."

"How long did she stay?"

"Somewhere around 7 o'clock."

"Was her attention called to your shoes?"

"Yes, I had them on my feet to go milk, and I throwed my foot out like that (indicating), and showed her my fine shoes that I had on."

"Was there any other pair of plow shoes in your house?"

"No sir, that was the only pair of plow shoes in the house."[6]

Slover took the stand again on cross-examination and was asked, "What size shoe do you wear?" Erwin placed defendant's shoes taken from him at the time of his arrest, beside those of Slover's.

Slover replied, "About the same as that I guess; ain't much difference."

"It would take an expert to find out whether they would fit your tracks, wouldn't it?" asked Erwin.

"Yes, I guess it would; I guess you would find a little difference in the track right here if nowhere else."

"You don't know the size of that shoe, do you?

"No sir," replied Slover.

"Was there any cast made of the track?" asked Erwin.

"Not that I know of."

"In other words the track was fit to the shoe and the shoe to the track at the same time?"

"Yes sir."

"Isn't that what is called a common plow shoe?" asked Erwin.

"It may be," replied Slover.

"Haven't you seen hundreds of them and aren't they commonly worn by the farmers in the country?"

"Not that I know of."

"You don't know the size?"

"No; 8 or 9 or 10," replied Slover. "All I know is it fit the track exactly."

Erwin established, through his line of questioning, that the direction of the trail of tracks left by the murderer, which Slover pointed out on the map at this trial, were definitely not the same ones nor in the same direction that he testified to at the preliminary examination in Lamberton.

Erwin asked, "You don't know how many people went through the yard the night before or the morning after the homicide?

"I don't."

"Did you go through there?"

"No sir," replied Slover.

The most damaging testimony given by Slover at this trial was that he now positively identified the defendant as the person who shot Lufkin.

"Don't you know, sir, that at the last term in this case, considerable stress was laid on the fact that you didn't recognize this man, the defendant, the night of August 18th when within 6 feet of you?" asked Erwin.

"Yes sir," replied Slover.

"Now haven't you changed your testimony to meet this demand?"

"No sir, I have not."

"Well, how can you explain your change of testimony, Mr. Slover?"

"I don't know that any person can word their testimony just exactly the same, without reading it over or being prompted, and I have neither read it over nor been prompted."

"On August 18th, you saw the defendant, his whole body, the shape of his head, with the exception of the handkerchief covering the sides of his neck -- his shoulders, his hands and his body? You didn't recognize him until he spoke to you?"

"No sir," said Slover.

"Now, 4 days afterward you saw a person 36 feet from you, looking out from a lighted room through a pane of glass into the darkness beyond, and you recognized that person by his back fleeing from you as William Rose?"

"Yes sir."[7]

If there was any reasonable doubt for a jury to consider, this last point brought out by the defense should have acquitted Rose, but this would not be the case.

⚜

A witness for the State, A.M. Grundin gave testimony on cross-examination by Erwin that was a bit perplexing:

Mr. Grundin stated that on August 22 he was helping his neighbor, Mr. Gustafson, stack grain when they saw someone riding a cream-colored pony pass close by, at about 5:00 p.m. They had stopped working to have a bit of lunch.

Erwin asked, "Do you think it was a man on horseback?"

"No," replied Grundin.

Erwin asked this same question three more times, and each time Mr. Grundin stated he did not think it was a man on horseback.

On redirect, Childs asked, "Was it a man or woman on the horse?"

Grundin replied, while shrugging his shoulders, "Must be a man?"[8]

Another witness for the State, Joseph Aldrich, testified that he had known the Rose family for eight or ten years.

On cross-examination Erwin asked, "Did you see the defendant before August 22nd and have a conversation with him?"

"Yes sir. It was about 15th of May 1888; we were going from my place to Tracy. I was driving a horse hitched to a cart; he was riding

55

a horse behind me most of the time. I asked him how that Lufkin slander suit was coming out.

"He says, 'Damn him, that will never bother him any; I'm going to shoot that son-of-a-bitch.'"

Erwin says, "How can you account for him saying that?"

"Well, he was rather given to that kind of language in a great many instances."

"So you took it as mere talk or bravado?"

"Yes sir."

"You didn't think it showed any danger to Lufkin?"

"Well, I don't think I should have been scared if he made that bluff to me."

"You thought it was idle talk?"

"Yes sir."

"Now, tell the jury, what do you mean by slander suits?"

"Mr. Lufkin commenced a suit against the Rose family and Mr. Averill."

"Did slander suits grow out of a prosecution of Lufkin for incest with his daughter, Grace Lufkin and his niece, Alice Sloan? Did you understand these slander suits grew out of public prosecution of Mr. Lufkin?"

"Yes sir."[9]

THE THIRD TRIAL

✦

Rose testified on his own behalf, part of his testimony follows:

"Where were you on Saturday the 18th of August, 1888?" asked Erwin.

Rose stated, "In the forenoon I was at home. About half past one or two o'clock I went to Tracy and purchased a box of cartridges from David Stafford. They were .44 Webleys and purchased them for my Uncle Tom.

"Then got on my pony and traveled north a ways and met a couple men who were working on a threshing machine. I asked them if they knew where the Lufkin tree claim was. One of the men pointed across and said, 'In that direction, you see those two knolls over there in the plowed field?'"

"I says, 'Yes sir.'"

"He says, 'That is on the Lufkin tree claim.' And he asked me if I was going to contest the claim."

"'Well,' I says, 'I don't know. We will see more about that further on.' And I asked him if he thought they could hold it."

"'Well,' he says, 'I don't know anything about it.' That was about all the conversation we had. It was about 5 or 6 o'clock by this time."

"We chatted for quite awhile and then I got on my pony and rode over to the tree claim. I rode over the entire claim and examined it, and then I headed for home. It was quite dark by this time and I got astray, and found myself near Slover's place."

"I rode up to the east barn door as Slover was coming out of the barn and said, 'Good evening, Mr. Slover.'"

"He was carrying a lantern and held it up pretty close to my face, about 3 or 4 feet away, and said, 'That's you is it Will?'"

"I asked him if I could put my horse in the barn and feed it."

"Mr. Slover said, 'Well sure, and go on and get some supper,' and I went to the house and had some lunch. Saw Mr. Lufkin in the room but we did not speak to each other."

"I told Mr. Slover I was in the area seeing a Mr. Casley about the $5 he owed me. I didn't care to let Mr. Slover know what I was really there for. After I finished lunch, Mr. Slover and I went out to the barn and he took me around and showed me his stock. After I watered my pony, I got on her and went home. Arrived home close to 12 o'clock."

Erwin asked, "What were your activities on August 22nd?"

"In the forenoon I worked on the buggy in the granary. I was cutting out tins to go over the hubs to keep the dirt out. After dinner, I went into the granary and painted those tins, and painted the end of the hub on the wheels, the outer end and the end of the tongue. They were painted black.

"After dinner I sawed some wood. Mother requested me to saw wood for her. Mr. Schultz and I went out into the yard and sawed wood. After that I went to the field with Mr. Schultz and got a load of grain about 1 o'clock. Came back with the load and then got my pony, took it to the barn and fed it.

"Then came into the house, took off my overalls and my plow shoes.

"I told mother I was going to Uncle Tom's, and I think she asked me what I was going for. And I told her what my errand was, and I think she asked if I couldn't put it off until some other time; and I told her 'No,' I had agreed to bring them over and I was going to do it. I was going to take my Uncle Tom a box of cartridges that I had bought from Mr. Stafford the Saturday before.

"I put on corduroy pants and 'gaiters,' placed the box of cartridges in my left hip pocket, my watch in the right hip pocket, and started for Uncle Tom's between 2 and 3 o'clock that day.

"I arrived at Uncle Tom's between 6 and 7 o'clock. He had moved from the Boomhauer place that afternoon to a farm nearby. I happened by accident to come upon it by noticing a red and white-spotted cow among the herd, that I once owned but sold to Mr. Simmons that spring. Mr. Simmons lived with Uncle Tom at the time. I rode to the house near where these cattle were, tied my pony to a tree and walked toward the house. At the door I recognized my aunt, Christine Rose and my cousin, Josephine Simmons.

"Shortly after I arrived, Uncle Tom and Frank Simmons got to the house with a wagon load. I helped them unload some lumber, a cupboard for the kitchen, and a couple of pigs.

"I then gave the box of cartridges to Uncle Tom. I visited with the family awhile and left about 8 o'clock towards home, arriving there close to 10 o'clock.

"I tied the pony to the picket rope, took the saddle and bridle and put them in the barn. When I got in the house I pulled off my shoes and went upstairs to bed. I undressed, put my night clothes on and came downstairs for lunch. Mother and Dora were in the main room at the time. I had a piece of pie, a piece of cake, a glass of milk and some tea and went back to bed."

"And what did you do on August 23rd?" asked Erwin.

"I got up between 5 and 6 o'clock, got dressed and went downstairs for breakfast. After that, I checked on the pony and fed her. Came back to the house and told Mother I was going to the bridge to look for my watch. It wasn't in my pocket when I dressed, so must've lost it when I stopped for 'nature's call' by the bridge on the way home last night.

"Got on my pony and headed for Willow Creek Bridge where I found the watch, just as I'd suspected. On the way home, I stopped at the Boomhauers expecting to find my uncle and cousin there to work on the place as I understood they had the place rented and there was still farm work to be done. Mrs. Boomhauer said they had moved on the previous day about a mile away and so I left and headed for home.

"I happened to come upon Mr. Turner and Mr. Kelly who were cutting flax and stopped to chat a bit.

"Mr. Turner said, 'There's somebody in this country that can shoot.'

"Mr. Kelly says, 'Why?'

"'Why haven't you heard? Lufkin was shot last night about 8 o'clock.'

"And I said, 'The hell you say.'

"Turner said, 'Yes, it's a fact, I got it pretty straight; just heard it from Mr. Mickelson.'

"About this time, I got on my pony and headed for home. Arrived home before dinner and told Mother what happened to Lufkin."[10]

An alibi would be Rose's defense. To prove this, witnesses were produced who testified that Rose was at his Uncle Tom's at the time of the murder and that he returned home that night, reaching there about 10 o'clock. It was likewise proved that Rose went to his uncle's the morning following the homicide.

Several absurdities developed at this trial: According to Rose's own testimony, he was four hours going to his uncle's on the day of the homicide, a distance of only 9 1/2 miles, and two hours in making the return trip, while the next morning, it took him only one hour to make it. Then too, he gave as his errand in going to his uncle's, that he went to take him a box of cartridges, and assigned no good reason for going there the following morning.

The falsity of the alibi was exposed by the testimony of Mrs. Boomhauer, a witness for the state, and by Rose's own statements. Rose's uncle had occupied a portion of the Boomhauer place until the afternoon of the homicide, when he moved with his family to a house one mile directly to the south.

At about 7:00 the next morning, Rose came to the Boomhauer place, dismounted from and hitched his pony, and went up to the portion of the house that his uncle had formerly occupied. Finding it vacant, walked around to the portion occupied by the Boomhauers, where he met Mrs. Boomhauer, by whom he was informed that his uncle had moved on the previous day, and pointed to the house to which he had moved.

Rose testified that he did not know that his uncle had moved when he left the house on the day of the homicide, and that he learned of it by accident.

After several days of testimony and closing arguments by the prosecution and defense attorneys, Judge Webber gave his rulings to the jury.

The judge's charge was clear and impartial and was read to the jury in such a deliberate and careful manner that they could not fail to grasp every point presented for their guidance and consideration.

When the spectators left the courtroom, the opinion most generally expressed was that there would be another disagreement. In about an hour Judge Webber was sent for, and the jury informed him that they had agreed upon a verdict.

When it was read and it was learned that they found "William Rose guilty of murder in the first degree, as charged in the indictment," the conclusion expressed the sentiments of those who heard it.

The usual motion for a new trial was made. In the afternoon, Judge Brown of Rose's counsel moved for an arrest of judgment, and asked the court to certify to the governor that there were such mitigating circumstances in the case as would justify his being imprisoned for life. Both these requests were overruled.[11]

Judge Webber then ordered the defendant to stand up and asked him if he had anything to say why sentence should not be passed upon him. He said he had, and continued as follows:

I have had a partial trial. The officers of the court have been combined against me; each officer has been a prosecuting attorney. Then turning to the large crowd present, and with a defiant wave of his hand, he added, In spite of this audience, and of you, I say I am as innocent of this crime, of which I am convicted as you are. That's all.[12]

Judge Webber stated to those in the courtroom that the trial had been impartial and fair, that it was the custom of convicted criminals to protest their innocence, and that the verdict of the jury was warranted by the evidence.

Judge Webber then passed sentence, "Rose is to be hanged by the neck until he is dead, within three months from the date of this sentence, at a time to be appointed by the governor."[13] Later, Governor Merriam fixed April 11, 1890 as the day of execution.

During these proceedings, the judge was visibly affected, while Rose was as cool and calm as he had been during all three trials of this case. The verdict of the jury and the sentence of the court met with popular approval.

Counsel for Rose informed the public that the motion for a new trial would be argued at New Ulm in February, 1890 and that if it was not granted, as it was not likely to be, the case would be appealed to the State Supreme Court.

It was of the opinion of those who knew Rose best that he would not weaken when the penalty of the law was inflicted upon him. Whatever Rose might be, he came from a stock of men who never lacked physical courage.

His father, James, served during the Civil War and participated in 26 battles. He was also commended for his bravery in the line of duty. He was wounded four times while in the service. His mother was a woman of wonderful nerve, and during the trials, never broke down until she heard of his conviction. As was to be expected, she firmly believed in her son's innocence.[14]

CHAPTER FOURTEEN
State Supreme Court Appeal

The appeal in the case of The State of Minnesota vs. William Rose was heard at the April Term of Court in 1891. Erwin and Wellington appeared for Rose, and Assistant Attorney General Childs and County Attorney Madigan, of Redwood County, appeared for the State.

The brief of the State presented a long chain of strong circumstantial evidence, the prosecution claiming that proof of guilt was never more convincingly established.

The following points brought by the prosecution are taken from court documents:

The defendant, William Rose, was at enmity with the deceased, Moses Lufkin, and that Rose manifested that enmity by threats of violence and other incidents.

That Rose left his father's residence between 2 and 3 o'clock on the afternoon of the homicide, riding a buckskin pony, wearing a slouched, light-colored cowboy hat, a short checkered coat, blue jean overalls, and heavy plow shoes.

That he was identified on the journey by at least five persons.

That his pony was identified by several persons familiar with it, and that a pony of that description, ridden by a man, was seen going that afternoon in the direction of Slover's by at least fourteen persons residing along the route between the defendant's home and the scene of the murder.

That tracks were found in the garden of the Slover place after the homicide, which conformed perfectly to the plow shoes worn that day by the defendant.

That tracks were found in the ravine and elsewhere in the neighborhood of the homicide, which exhibited the same peculiarities found to be characteristic of the foot of the pony.

That a clay spot was found on the defendant's shoes resembling clay found in the ravine.

That the death was affected by a shot from a rifle, and that the ball was homemade; that the defendant was in possession of or had access to a rifle, and of molds, which cast the same size of ball that killed the deceased, and that Rose had cast balls with said mold.

That early on the morning following the evening of the murder, the pony was found tethered near the barn of James Rose, the father of the defendant, appearing to be jaded, and evincing the strongest proof that it had been severely overdriven.

That immediately after, officers, Craig and Segar, visited the Rose place on the morning following the murder that Rose mounted the pony and rode it across country -- mainly across lots -- in the direction of Calvin Boomhauer's house, where he called and engaged in conversation with Mrs. Boomhauer.

That the alibi on which defendant relied on was overcome by evidence of the most conclusive character.

Rose's defense responded to these allegations with the following points:

It was clearly known throughout the community that Rose was not on friendly terms with Lufkin, but never posed any verbal threats or bodily harm against him.

On the afternoon of the homicide, the defendant mounted his pony and rode to his uncle's to deliver a box of cartridges and remained there until 8 o'clock that evening.

That day he wore a narrow brimmed hat and light colored gaiters; not plow shoes. There was clearly much discrepancy in witness testimony as to the clothing worn by the man riding a cream-colored pony and that this pony was seen by so many witnesses and traveling in different directions; clearly showed that there was more than one cream-colored pony in the county.

A man's tracks found near Slover's residence the following morning were said to fit the defendant's plow shoes, but many people were out looking for tracks that morning, traipsing back and forth. They placed different shoes in the tracks, making the tracks an unreliable point of evidence.

And the tracks of the horse were those of one not shod. The defendant's horse was shod in the front.

The clay found in the defendant's plow shoes that were taken from him on the day of his arrest at Montgomery's farm, was from wet mud from a new well being dug on the Montgomery property.

The rifle used in the homicide was a common caliber easily owned by anyone, and none of the witnesses saw the defendant carrying a weapon.

The defendant enjoyed riding his pony for long hours across the prairie. As the pony was seldom grain fed, it tired easily and was in poor health, and this could certainly explain its jaded appearance.

Important witness testimony for the defense was brought forth by John Averill, a neighbor of the Rose family. Averill stated that while at Lufkin's funeral, Slover said, "I don't know if I have the right man."

And another nearby neighbor, Mary Potter testified that she saw a man on a cream-colored pony on the day of the homicide, but it was "a stranger and clearly not William."

All of these points should have clearly caused "reasonable doubt" in the minds of the jury, but regrettably, this was not the case.

Relative to instructions of the court, that errors were alleged, Judge Webber instructed the jury as follows:

"If certain facts and circumstances satisfied their minds beyond a reasonable doubt, that defendant was guilty, that he might be convicted upon such circumstantial evidence, that it is not necessary that each and every circumstance should be proved. It is in vain that we attempt to detect and punish crime unless we resort to circumstantial evidence. This you are to decide upon the evidence before you and nothing else."₁

After some deliberation, the jury upheld the lower court's decision of a guilty verdict.

CHAPTER FIFTEEN
U.S. Supreme Court Appeal

The Clifton Holden case went to the U.S. Supreme Court on a technical point that also bore on the Rose case, and it was stipulated between the prosecution and the defense that no further action would be taken in the Rose case until the U.S. Supreme Court had given an opinion in the case against Holden.[1]

In December 1890, the U.S. Supreme Court gave its decision in the Holden case. It declared that the John Day Smith Law passed in 1889 and commonly called "the midnight assassination law," was held to be constitutional.

This "law" designated the mode of punishment, in that it prescribed executions must take place before sunrise, the prisoner was to be held in solitary confinement, there would be a limit to the number of persons to be present at hangings (especially reporters), and newspapers were forbidden to publish more than a mere statement that any person was hanged -- and that, as there was no saving clause in the new law, one could not be held under the old law.[2]

The Rose case was appealed to the U.S. Supreme Court on the grounds of insufficient evidence to justify the verdict, but the U.S. Supreme Court upheld the lower court's decision, stating that no errors were committed in the case.

Judge Vanderburgh affirmed Judge Webber's decision with the following statement:

Under the statutes of the state, it is not improper for the court in its charge to review and analyze the evidence. It is not error for the court to state to the jury that certain evidence is material or that it tends to prove certain facts or to comment upon the testimony when it is done fairly and the jury is fully advised of their duty and responsibility in the premises.

Where, upon an indictment for murder, evidence of threats and the exhibition of malice by the accused against the deceased is introduced on behalf of the state, the defendant may contradict or explain such evidence but may not in extenuation or justification introduce independent evidence of instances of personal immorality on the part of the deceased or his general bad character. The evidence presented was considered and held sufficient to justify the verdict.[3]

At this time, there was a concerted movement to induce Governor Merriam to commute the death sentence in the Rose case. Every possible legal relief was resorted to, but every effort proved futile.

A number of petitions from the people of Redwood, Lyon, and Murray counties asking for commutation of the sentence of William Rose to life imprisonment were received by the governor.

In August 1891, Rose wrote the following letter to the governor, pleading for clemency:

To Hon. W.R. Merriam, Governor of the State of Minnesota,

Sir: Standing as I do, convicted of the highest crime known to the law, and being desirous of a commutation of sentence, I make this petition and pray for clemency. I am wholly innocent of the crime of killing Moses L. Lufkin, and I believe that in time I will be able to establish my innocence before the world. In order that I may do so I humbly ask that the sentence of the court be commuted to imprisonment.

William Rose[4]

On August 13, 1891, a formal petition of the jury that found the prisoner guilty, asked that a life sentence be imposed. This was signed by jurors W.D. Smith, Lewis Halznagel, S.S. Dalson, C.T. Waterman, H.C. Christopherson, D.L. Flazier, James Arnold, Alex McLeod, T. L. Hiatt, and A.H. Anderson. Juror Sever Ferring had gone to California, and O.A. Hines refused to sign.₅

Separate petitions of residents from Redwood, Murray, and Lyon counties all claimed acquaintance with Rose, and called upon the governor to secure executive clemency on this case.

One of the most interesting letters received by the governor came from Mr. Thayer, an architect from Mankato, who owned lands adjacent to the homes of Lufkin and Rose, and was well-acquainted with both. Rose had been in his employ for a long time and had lived at Thayer's house. Mr. Thayer felt well-qualified to vouch for the young man's character:

Mr. Rose was a good, kind-hearted, generous, young man, and could not have been guilty of this crime. Lufkin was a man who was universally distrusted and despised. He had family difficulties, and his wife left him before he came from the state of Maine. I cannot remember all of the particulars of his history that he related to me at different times when I stayed with him on my way to and from my place, but I do remember it was a mixture of fast horses, legal difficulties, and troubles concerning his wife.

I remember distinctly how he told me years before he had any difficulty with the Rose family that he expected to die a violent death, and I understand from his talk, he was afraid some of his old enemies would kill him. He also made the statement that if it were not for the girl, as he called his daughter, Minnie, he would put an end to his existence.

Lufkin had a vile nature, low moral condition and was considered a dangerous man. He was a disturber of the peace of the community and was killed by some other person whom he had more deeply wronged than he had William Rose, seems to me very probable.

The marriage of Lufkin's daughter, Grace, to a young man in the neighborhood, that man's desertion of her and disappearance from the country on account of some family difficulty previous to the murder, are things that might throw light on the murderer if carefully investigated.[6]

A Sleepy Eye lawyer, J.M. Thompson, wrote at length reviewing the history of the case. He stated that from his position and intimacy with the facts and people, he was in a position to give a correct diagnosis of the public temper. He knew that a great majority of the people of Redwood County would be glad to know that the death penalty in this case was not to be executed:

He recited the fact that Rose was tried three times before a conviction was had. The last trial occurred during the most intense excitement over another murder in Redwood County.

The jury in the first case stood 8 to 4 in favor of acquittal, and at one time during the balloting, it was 10 to 2. The jury in the second trial stood 7 to 5, and at one time stood 9 to 3 for acquittal. Thus 19 of the jurors had voted not guilty after hearing the evidence.

As stated, the third trial was held during a storm of excitement. When Frank Dodge's dead body was found, had it not been for the salutary influence of an open court and the presence of Judge Webber, there's no doubt that people would have entered the jail and taken out both Rose and Holden and lynched them. The press and public sentiment cried out for a conviction. The county was becoming burdened by the costs of trials, and the verdict of guilty was found.[7]

A *Tribune* reporter went to Governor Merriam's summer residence at Forest Lake to ascertain what had been decided upon, and it is presented as follows:

I have received a number of personal letters asking that the sentence be made a life one, and also a petition, quite liberally signed, asking the same thing, but I have not taken any action in the matter, said Governor Merriam.

This week I will give it some consideration. I want to review the testimony in the case before I come to any conclusion. That is the only way I can form a just opinion as to whether I should interfere with the sentence of the court or not. Judge Brown has been to see me, but I have not given the matter any attention and, as I say, will not do so until I review the evidence this week.[8]

It turned out that Governor Merriam did not reverse the judge's decision, and Sheriff Charlie Mead of Redwood Falls was given instructions to proceed with the preparations for the execution of Rose as planned. The governor fixed the date of execution for October 16, 1891 and refused to interfere further.

CHAPTER SIXTEEN
No Fear of Death

One would think that the knowledge of certain death would cause a man to lose spirit and strength, but such was not the case with William Rose, doomed to atone for the murder of Moses Lufkin.

To look at Rose, he had the same hope, the same good feeling, and the same air of disregard that he had when the prospects of commutation were brightest. He knew that he was to hang and that the governor would not reverse his former stand, but it did not appear to move him in the least.

In conversation with a reporter, Rose stated that he had not lost any sleep, did not dream any, and had not noticed a change in his robust appetite.

He was seated comfortably in his cell with a novel in his hands and smiling pleasantly. The only thing he had to complain of, he said, was the refusal of the jailers to allow him to read *The Review* and other newspapers. He had not been permitted to see a news journal for weeks and he could see no reason why he should be prevented from reading the comments of the press about his case.[1]

∽◌◌◌

Rose's last days in New Ulm were trying ones, but he still remained optimistic. He wrote the following letter on October 11, 1891, and it appeared in *The New Ulm Review* to show his appreciation of all the work done for him by the New Ulm people:

I wish to say to the citizens of New Ulm that I kindly thank them for the noble effort they have made on my behalf. As the time is drawing near when I shall be led forth to my doom, if his Excellency does not heed your earnest and just request, the only thing I can say for myself is that I am wrongfully accused and maliciously convicted.

Yes, I assert this in the face of all the conflicting circumstances, and, if I must die for another's crime, so be it. And while thanking you all for all you have endeavored to do for me, I especially desire to thank Sheriff Schmelz and his wife for their kindness during the former's term of office, as well as to ex-sheriff Schmid and wife and to the jailer, for they have all been very kind to me.

I do this through the columns of your paper because it is the only way in which they may know that one and all receive my thanks. Again expressing my innocence, I will bid you all good-bye, hoping you may never again be called upon to perform such a duty as now falls to your lot.

Asking God's blessing and trusting that I may yet meet you all, I will close.

Yours sincerely, William Rose[2]

The following night, October 12, Rose wrote a letter that appeared in *The St. Paul Weekly Pioneer Press* on October 15, attempting to show that the evidence against him was circumstantial and stating his position:

The time has now arrived when I feel justified in taking this step. I wish to inform the public of the atrociousness of the proceedings and also that I affirm my innocence of all knowledge of the crime charged to me.

It appears as though Redwood County has been afflicted with the crime of murder, and four have been done within the same number of years, but I ask, does it follow that someone must hang? To go back to the beginning it would take more of an adept person than I to follow all the phases.

False presentations and back thrusts have been hurled at me in the face of a court of justice, but I wish to give to the public the main features of the case as it came out at my three different trials.

First, there was or appeared to be, a case of an alleged bomb or hell machine, as the deceased named it. The alleged bombing should have been done on the 14th of June, 1887. At that time, I was staying with my father on the farm cornering with the deceased's farm, and remained with my father till the middle of August, when I went to Dakota to look after my property there and to thrash during the fall, but returned to my father's house by November 1st of the same year and there remained the rest of the winter.

During the winter, or rather the month of February 1888, my father, brother, and brother's wife, caught the deceased in criminal intimacy with his niece. Consequently, he was arrested for the crime of incest, but before the examination, or ten days after his arrest, the alleged bombing came to light, and I was arrested and charged with arson.

Notwithstanding, the arson offense was committed June 14, 1887; the arrest was not made till February 12, 1888. The deceased had repeatedly told me that he did not know whom to accuse, and the proof he had was a Chicago InterOcean newspaper, which he procured from a stake used to mark out a line fence. I will add that the grand jury failed to find a bill against either party.

The deceased sold his farm sometime in May 1888 and moved to Eli Slover's on the Cottonwood River in Redwood County where he met his death.

Skipping to August 22, 1888, on the afternoon of that day, I, the accused, went to my uncle's place, starting from my father's, and remaining at my uncle's till about 8 pm, arriving at home at 10 pm.

Returning again to my uncle's on the morning of the 23rd, I remained there till 1 pm, when I returned home again, and on the morning of the 24th, I went to stack hay, as agreed, for Levi Montgomery where I was arrested.

Then on the 30th of August, 1888, the examination at Lamberton occurred before Justice of the Peace, Joseph E. Libby. Now you observe only eight days intervened between the murder and the examination and all attempts at identification were a failure, except John Furgeson and George Robbins, who saw me one mile from home on my road to my uncle's.

But Eli Slover saw a man at 8:15 pm some sixty or eighty feet, running in the shade of four rows of willows that were twenty feet high and Slover testified, "He had his back to me and was bending forward and running very fast, but I took it to be William Rose."

"You will not swear positively it was him," asked the attorney.

"No, I could not," replied Slover.

Then at the November term of court, the county attorney, in his opening address, drew a graphic picture of a man on the side of a barn and solemnly affirmed that the defendant had been repeatedly caught shooting at that man with a revolver and that when questioned, said that I was practicing so I could hit that man in the heart and that I was going to shoot "old man Lufkin".

Observe the absurdity of such a remark, and I need not tell you no such thing was ever proven or attempted. Eli Slover saw the man again and still took it to be William Rose, but was not sure. I ask how could he be in the face of five positive eye witnesses. The result of the trial, after a deliberation of four days and five nights, was a disagreement of eight to four in favor of defendant.

Again at the spring term of court at Redwood, the county attorney in airing his oratory said:

Your honor and gentlemen of the jury, I intend to prove that this defendant, while confined at New Ulm, did set fire to the jail intending to try and make his escape, periling the lives of five other fellow prisoners.

Again observe the absurdity and the failure to prove the same. Anyone can see it at a glance that an attempt to poison the minds of the jury, and the court, could be his only motive.

Then after a trial lasting over two weeks, Eli Slover again seeing that man in the shade but this time, he thought it was William Rose. Result of trial after a deliberation of four days, another disagreement of seven to five in favor of the defendant.

Then, to recall it to your memory, during the second trial, someone caused to be published a report that it did not make any difference whether a conviction was secured or not; that in the event of a failure to convict, the defendant would be taken back to Dakota and there tried for the murder of his wife, a half-breed Indian, from whom he received $18,000 and his famous buckskin pony. But there happened to be a man there, a neighbor of mine and a former resident of Redwood who promptly told them it was a "damned lie."

I ask why such reports? Then another six months intervened and the last and final trial, when Eli Slover saw the man again and knew him to be William Rose and was positive of it, although at neither of the former trials was he certain of it, but on the cross-examination of Cy Wellington, he admitted he was deeply interested in securing a conviction and wanted to see the defendant convicted if he was guilty.

But at the last trial there was no doubt about it; he (Slover) saw William Rose and knew it was he all the time, and intended to testify as such.

In the month of May 1888, the deceased sold a farm taking in exchange therefore $1100 or $1000 cash and a farm near a witness for $800. Then the deceased mortgaged a second farm for $1000 giving him $2000 in cash when he moved in with the Slovers.

Then some few days before the 22nd of August, 1888, the date of the homicide, the deceased received a pension of $1500 from the United States government, making $3500.

Now the homicide. Then follows the failure to account for that money and the attempt by my attorney to bring the money question up against the witness in court.

I do not claim friendship with the deceased and never did, simply because he was a most perfidious scoundrel. Nothing appeared too low for him. Although I have worked for him very often and attended him when he was sick, I have never spent a night in his house, nor made him a friendly call, and I don't think any moral-minded man would. He has repeatedly told me that he was afraid for his life, as he had enemies among his wife's folks that would kill him if they ever got a chance.

And again, he had a son-in-law who married his daughter after only a few days acquaintance, and only one week of quiet and happiness was their lot, when the deceased drove his son-in-law from his paternal roof at the point of a revolver at 12 o'clock at night, reminding him that he would shoot him if he ever saw him again.

The son-in-law replied, "If you shoot me before I do you, it is all right."

I do not attribute the crime to the son-in-law, nor do I think Grace had anything to do with it, but I do think I know who the guilty man is, and lots of others think as I do. Circumstances point strongly to him, if positive proof is lacking.

All the proof they have is circumstantial but a conviction was returned and sentence passed, not realizing they were condemning an innocent man to the gallows; and all the appeals have been taken without effect, and last, his Excellency refuses to commute the sentence of the lower court, and an innocent man is condemned to swing.

Words fail me to point out the prejudice and unfairness of such proceedings, and my regret at leaving this world in such a light would be hard to picture.

To think of my poor mother, realizing as she does of her son's inno-cence, and realizing that on the 16th of October, he will be launched into eternity for another felon's crime.

Oh God, forbid that such shall be permitted. If I were guilty of the crime charged to me, hanging would be my just reward, but to think of such a thing, being innocent, nearly drives me frantic, and the real criminal gloating over my downfall and enjoying his gains, while his hands are red with the blood of another man's.

My attorneys have made a hard fight and a long one. Their equal is not to be found on the criminal calendar of Minnesota, and I appre-ciate their noble efforts and the efforts all my friends have made on my behalf, and kindly thank them.

Especially I wish to thank F.S. Brown, the junior counsel in the case, and ex-sheriff Schmid and his wife. My praises of them cannot be too high for their treatment of me, and the present Sheriff, L.H. Schmelz and wife, also receive my thanks for their kindness.

Again, I will say the only regret that I have at leaving this world is the thought of my friends and parents. In conclusion, I will say that if I have to leave this world at the end of a rope, I warn you, one and all, to watch the man I have spoken of, and the time will come when you will all be convinced of his guilt as I am.

Yours truly, William Rose₃

The friends of Rose were loath to abandon him to his fate, and on the morning of October 14, Judge Brown again called on Governor Merriam, accompanied by Senator Peterson, Andrew Eckstein of New Ulm, and Senator Davis of St. Peter, asking that Rose's sentence be commuted.

Judge Brown made quite an argument in favor of commutation. Senator Peterson's talk was short but earnest. Senator Peterson stated that he did not believe Rose should be hanged. The evidence was circumstantial and he would just as soon believe that others had committed the crime as to think that Rose was the guilty man.

The senator further stated that he had been in Renville County a number of times during the summer, and the sentiment was entirely in favor of commuting the sentence of the condemned man. The locals felt that suspicion rested on other parties in the community, and that the sheriff's department had failed to properly investigate the murder or interrogate other suspects; therefore an innocent man was condemned to the gallows.[4]

The governor told the gentlemen frankly that he would not interfere in any way -- that the letter of Judge Webber stating that the trial was conducted fairly in every way settled the case, and Rose would meet his fate soon. With this, the petitioners were obliged to content themselves, but still felt a great injustice had been done.[5]

That same afternoon, Governor Merriam received a telegram from some notable citizens of Redwood Falls, signed by W.D. Flinn, H.D. Baldwin, C.N. George, O.L. Dornberg, E.D. French, and W.P. Dunnington asking for a stay of 30 days in the execution of the sentence of Rose. These same names were attached to a dispatch to Assistant Attorney General Childs, which went as follows: "We have wired the governor for a stay of Rose's sentence of 30 days. Will you please see him on time?" Mr. Childs was out of the city at the time, but on a previous occasion stated he would not oppose the changing of the death penalty for Rose, to imprisonment for life."[6]

CHAPTER SEVENTEEN
Last Day in New Ulm

Wednesday, October 14, 1891 was perhaps the most trying day that Rose experienced, and yet he displayed a fortitude and nerve that were remarkable. For several days before, he had been constantly and acutely reminded of his fate.

First there was a visit from his mother, which was exceedingly affecting and which caused Rose to weep like a child; then his father and sisters called upon him, and at 2:20 pm his attorney wired him that all hope was gone. That was the most critical period of his great trial, but by great force of will he resigned himself to his fate and showed no signs of weakening.

Shortly after he received the news from his attorney, he sent for Reverend Meske of the New Ulm Congregational Church. The clergyman remained for upwards of an hour, and in the evening spent half an hour with the condemned man. Rose spoke freely with the reverend and stated that he had no fear of death. His trust in God was strong and his innocence strengthened him.[1]

"I don't want the idea to go out," he said, "that I refuse to see ministers. I'm not a heathen by any means. I will gladly see any who call. I have made no arrangements for any to be present when I am hanged, but they are welcome if they choose to come."

"And your belief is --?"

"Presbyterian," interrupted Rose.[2]

At 5 o'clock, a *Review* reporter visited him and they conversed for quite some time. Asked as to how he felt, he laughed heartily and replied that he had passed the day agreeably. Then the action of the governor was referred to, and the prisoner, with an air of unconcern, said that such was life. He then went on to repeat the story given recently in the *Pioneer Press*, reasserting his innocence and accusing Eli Slover of the murder. He added that the letter, published in the *Pioneer Press* and written by himself, was "straight goods," and that the facts would someday appear as clearly to others as they did to him.

"Do you have any dread of death?" the reporter asked.

"No, why should I?" he answered. "An innocent man should never be afraid to die. And let me tell you again, I am innocent of this crime. I can hold my head as high as you or anyone else, even under present circumstances."

"But all men have some fear of death," said the reporter.

"Well if you have," said Rose, "you are a hypocrite."

Then referring to an article which recently appeared in the *Review* about the sympathetic ladies of Redwood Falls, he said that soon they would have an opportunity to cover him with sweet flowers without coming to New Ulm. With that he laughed and bid the reporter good-bye.₃ That night he went to bed as usual and slept well.

It was in the early morning hours of October 15th that a *Globe* correspondent arrived at the New Ulm Depot. This would be Rose's final interview as reported in the *St. Paul Daily Globe*, October 16, 1891 edition:

The *Globe* reporter was accompanied by State Senator Peterson and Attorney Joseph Eckstein. The reporter noted that the Brown County Jail was something of a model structure and harbored criminals from many counties. The jail was located opposite Congressman Lind's residence a short distance from the New Ulm Depot.

Lights were seen flickering in the jailhouse windows as the trio left the train depot and climbed the hill to the jail. The two-story brick structure, with tall, round-topped windows and a triple-arcade entrance displayed an Italianate influence. The numerous prominent chimneys reflected the lack of central heating.

After the three men arrived at the jail's entrance and knocked on the large, wooden door; Sheriff Schmelz greeted the visitors and welcomed them inside. Sheriff Mead was asleep on the second floor and was not disturbed for an hour, but in the meantime they were greeted by Jailer, John Schapekahm, who for three years had kept watch and ward over the condemned man.

Schapekahm told the reporter, "It is not for me to say whether he is innocent or guilty. I, personally, think him innocent."

Sheriff Mead finally appeared and granted the *Globe* newspaper man a final interview with Rose. Mead was a striking looking man, tall, slender, with gray moustache and keen of eye. The reporter fully explained his mission to the sheriff, and with a courtesy almost unprecedented, Mead gave him full power to do as he pleased, and allowed Rose to speak as he pleased. So the *Globe* correspondent, along with the jailer, were the only occupants of the jail corridor, as the latter rapped upon the iron bars with his bunch of keys.

"All right," said a sleepy voice.

While the key was turning in the lock, Rose jumped up, put on a pair of trousers and stepped into the glare of the corridor. There he stood in trousers and deep blue flannel shirt, looking the perfect gentleman.

"Good morning," Rose said, cheerfully, without waiting for an introduction to the stranger.

Like an athlete, Rose stepped across the corridor to where a pile of new clothing waited upon a little table. He knew that his death shroud was there, and so did the two men watching. Then, as if forgetful, he turned, and in trembling tones, Jailer Schapekahm introduced the newspaper man to Rose.

Rose then excused himself, stepped over to the little sink, turned on the water, and bathed face and neck. In the midst of it, he stopped, in answer to a query, and said:

"I shall say nothing at the last. What can an innocent man say?"

Then he splashed in the water a bit, used a towel vigorously, and began to put on his grave clothes. He knew the meaning of the new suit of black and shirt of darkest blue, kindly provided by Sheriff Schmelz, which he picked up for Rose to wear in his final days, and so did the two men with him.

But Rose dressed as if for a carnival, yet with the utmost deliberation, and without a tremor visible. And soon he stood, as courtly and graceful as if welcoming guests to his own home.

"In the published letter I wrote," he said to the *Globe* man, "two names were omitted. I blamed County Attorney Madigan for false representations -- representations he couldn't prove -- and another man I charged with the murder. I am innocent. I cannot make a confession when I have none to make."

Rose was told that Senator Peterson and Attorney Joseph Eckstein were waiting outside, but were too overcome with emotion to see him, and wished the reporter to tell Rose what they had tried to do to help him in his final hours.

"I thank them heartily," he said, "and you. I know they have done all they could."

Rose was dressed. He straightened his dark blue tie -- the little streaks of white upon it, the only relieving touch in his whole dress -- put on a new, soft, felt hat of black, a hat with broad brim and high crown, and William Rose was ready for his trip toward the gallows.

Deputy Sheriff Olmstead, of Redwood, then came into the corridor. He had been the night guard of Rose ever since the governor fixed the day of execution. Sheriff Mead also stepped inside the iron door. The deputy took from his little satchel a pair of handcuffs.

"You have no overcoat, Rose?" asked Sheriff Mead.

"No," said Rose.

"Schmelz," called Mead through the iron door, "will you loan me an overcoat for today?"

The New Ulm sheriff then quickly brought his own great fur coat and Rose donned it. He then put on a pair of fawn-colored gloves, and held out both hands to Deputy Olmstead. The latter only put one nipper on -- about the right wrist of Rose, and closed the other on his own left arm.

The iron door opened; Rose and Olmstead stepped through. To the left, in an open doorway of the sheriff's home, and part of the jail, stood Mrs. Schmelz. Rose extended his left hand.

"I thank you," he said to the weeping woman. "You have done very much for me, and I thank you."

The hall leading to the front entrance was crowded, but to only one did Rose respond as they spoke.

"We did all we could," said Attorney Eckstein, huskily.

"I know it. I thank you," responded Rose.

He was almost at the door. "Good-bye," he called, and Rose, Sheriff Mead, Deputy Olmstead and the *Globe* correspondent, stepped out into the darkness.₄

At the foot of the long flight of steps, an omnibus waited. Into this the four stepped, soon followed by Sheriff Schmelz. Not a word was spoken until the bus started. Then Rose fumbled in the pockets of the big overcoat with his left hand, produced a long cigar, and asked for a match.

It was the first time Rose had been in the free air for nearly three years. Yet he rode along as nonchalantly as a drummer on a late night train. He remarked how some of the carbons in the incandescent light had burned yellow, and gave it, as his sage opinion; that they were no better than a candle, only they didn't burn out.

Then in the chill of the darkened hour of morning, the little party was left at the deserted depot, and Sheriff Schmelz drove back to the jail. Probably a dozen curiosity seekers gathered to see Rose on his final trip from New Ulm.

While patiently waiting for the train to arrive, the four men conversed quietly in the cold morning air. Rose was gazing at the stars in the dark sky and was mesmerized by the bright full moon. In the distance, they heard the train chugging down the tracks, and it wasn't long before the whistle sounded and the light from the engine cast shadows along the depot platform. The train finally chugged to a stop. A few passengers departed with their luggage and several sacks of mail were left on the platform.

Rose was not anxious to board the train and took his time puffing on the cigar. Some curiosity seekers, who were Rose supporters, walked up to him, shook his hand, and wished him well. Several women brought him flowers and prayed with him before he boarded the train.

Finally the conductor shouted, "All aboard." Rose and the three gentlemen somberly entered the passenger car and found comfortable seating. Only a few other passengers boarded at the time.

On the fifteen-mile train ride to Sleepy Eye, Rose, the sheriffs, and the reporter attracted little attention as they sat in the smoker, gossiping as any traveling party might do. Other newspaper men were dozing in the sleeper, having come straight through from St. Paul, and even Judge Brown, who pleaded Rose's case before the governor, did not get up to see him.

The train arrived at Sleepy Eye at about 5:30 am, and the party alighted on the side opposite from the depot platform. They walked unobserved to the Commercial Hotel, only a block away, and were given the parlor on the first floor.

Then in an hour, for the first time, correspondents of the other papers appeared clamoring for news. Rose continued in the best of spirits, but his face, in the growing light, looked haggard and strained.

At 8 o'clock, he sat down to his last breakfast upon earth and was given the seat at the head of the table. Breakfast consisted of a bunch of grapes, a large beefsteak, oatmeal, German fried potatoes, a piece of toast, and a cup of coffee. His handcuffs were removed.

To his right sat the sheriff, to his left the deputy. Newspaper men filled out the table. The shadow of the gallows was upon all, yet it was a merry breakfast. Rose ate heartily, gave jest for jest, and was, in truth, king of the feast.

After breakfast, and for two hours, Rose sat in the hotel lobby unshackled and unrestrained talking with whom he pleased. He had a long conversation with J.C. Geiger of New Ulm, who was formerly one of the death watches. Rose told him that "it didn't make any difference, they could hang him, but they couldn't take his grit away from him." He told Sheriff Mead and others some humorous anecdotes of Colonel Sam McPhail, a great Minnesota eccentric, whom Rose knew well.

A short time later, Rose invited a news reporter to a chair, lighted a cigar, and offered the reporter one. After a few puffs, and without any leading up to it, Rose began to talk of the refusal of Governor Merriam to commute the sentence.

"I consider Governor Merriam," he said, "one of the most unfair men on earth. We met when he was not governor. It was on the banks of Lake Kampeska, South Dakota. He was with a hunting party and requested me to do a petty service for him. I refused and he insulted me, and I resented that insult. He probably remembered that incident when he refused to pardon me, an innocent man. I am innocent and some day the world may know it."

"Were you ever arrested?" asked one reporter.

"Yes, I was arrested twice; once for larceny and once for assault and battery, but both charges were dropped," said Rose.₅

Sitting in the hotel lobby, Rose shook hands and chatted gaily with old Sleepy Eye acquaintances, and if the main subject was spoken of, Rose would insist that fate was terrible, not to him, but to Minnesota, the authorities of which, he said, were about to execute an innocent man.

"Knowing myself innocent, death has no terrors for me, and what can an innocent man say?" was the way Rose answered a personal acquaintance, after which he quickly changed the subject.[6]

The train was late in leaving Sleepy Eye and quite a crowd was attracted, but Rose paid no heed. Rose was once again handcuffed to Deputy Olmstead and the two boarded the train taking two seats near the open door. A morbid curiosity seeker from the crowd stood on the car platform with a large coil of rope on his arm, intently gazing at Rose. About this time, Conductor Hughes appeared on the scene and hollered at the man, "Get the hell outa here you damn scoundrel." The man ran away laughing.[7] Rose told Mr. Hughes afterwards that the rope did not bother him, nor did the crowd of curiosity seekers making unsavory remarks, affect him in the least.

On the long train ride to Redwood, Rose talked and reminisced about his life out West. Then he asked that all the newspaper men on the train be summoned that he might make his statement:

Some people say that I was born in the Wild West, but my place of birth was in Pike County, Illinois, on January 8, 1861. Directly after the war I moved with my parents to Fillmore County, Minnesota, residing there until the fall of 1874, when we moved to Murray County, where my father now resides.

In the spring of 1884, I went to Campbell County, South Dakota, took a homestead and remained on same until the spring of 1887, when I returned to my Murray County home.

Nine years ago last June; I took a pleasure trip to the Pacific Coast. I don't hope for anything from the governor. I think I am going to hang and am ready. I am willing to see a spiritual advisor at Redwood, but have no statement to make, except that I am innocent.

My father called on me Monday and my mother and sisters Tuesday and I don't expect to see them again because I requested them to

89

*remain away from Redwood Falls. My brother, who I have not seen
for a year, will probably see me at Redwood.*[8]

At every stop along the route there were crowds of the morbidly
curious. When Redwood Falls was reached a hundred were upon the
platform, but Rose shackled to the deputy, was so quickly inside a closed
omnibus that few observed. During the mile drive to the town, Rose
looked eagerly out the front window, smoking a cigarette, and talking
freely.

"She looms up big," he said as the new courthouse came into view.[9]

In back of this, in the very heart of Redwood Falls, was the so-called
jail. It was nothing more than a little two-story frame cottage, 12 x 12
feet. The interior, dark and gloomy, was painted a depressing maroon,
and was lighted by two small grated windows high up. Sweat box is the
only name to apply to the prison.

As the bus drew up to the jail, there were 200 curious men and boys
lining the street. The bus was backed close to the open jail door, and all
were rushed inside in an instant.

Once inside, Rose threw off his coat, tossed it upon the narrow bed,
remarking, "Well, I'll see you again in the afternoon," and the wooden
door locked him in.

At noon, an excellent dinner was sent Rose from the Commercial
Hotel, and he ate heartily. The Commercial Hotel was located in the
heart of the city and within one block of the courthouse. The hotel was
three stories high, contained thirty-five rooms and had all the modern
conveniences; including steam heat, electric lights, hot and cold water
and even long distance telephone service. It was the pride of the city and
well known for its scrumptious meals and meticulous rooms.

At 1 o'clock, at his request, Sheriff Mead brought Reverend John
Sinclair, a spiritual adviser and Presbyterian minister, to Rose's cell. He
found him sitting on the cot looking quite cheery. Rose wished to con-
verse about himself.

"I have been maliciously lied against and maliciously convicted and will die an innocent man," declared Rose. "It is better to die with a conscience of innocence than to die making ten thousand confessions of guilt. I am prepared to die and know I am innocent."[10]

The reverend spent about an hour with him and in their conversation, Rose maintained his innocence and talked feelingly of his mother. He said he dreaded the ignominy of his death, but he was guiltless and would face the end with a clear conscience. He was prepared for the future; his trust was in the Lord, to whom he looked for salvation. The reverend then asked him if he wished to pray. Rose instantly fell on his knees on the cold, bare floor, and together they pled to the Lord for mercy and pardon.

When he arose, tears were in his eyes and his voice was husky with emotion. The reverend then prayed that the Lord would purge Rose of his sins, if he had any, as the Lord and Rose alone knew whether the latter was guilty. An attempt was made to have Rose make a confession, but the latter replied that he had nothing to confess. From this time on his demeanor seemed changed; his spirit of joking evidently left him and he realized more fully the awfulness of the approaching hour.

In the afternoon Rose requested the sheriff bring him a white shirt to wear for his photograph later that day. The sheriff obliged and Rose removed his heavy woolen shirt and slipped into the cool, crisp, white one. He put on a collar and black cravat and left the tiny jail cell for an afternoon of personal duties.

Rose appeared on the street, accompanied with the sheriff and deputy. A crowd of people followed him about in silent curiosity. Rose gazed upon the open air, the broad green fields and the throngs of people with seeming indifference and smiled at the faces peering through the windows at him. At the outspoken jeers of some ladies, he spoke in contempt and walked along the street with his head held high.

The three men entered J. Melges' barber shop on Main Street, where Rose sat for a shave and trim. He wanted a neat appearance before photos were taken at N.B. Anderson's Studio a short distance away.

Upon entering the long, narrow barber shop, Rose counted six barbers, each one standing alongside six black, leather barber chairs lined up along one wall, with large mirrors the entire length of the room. Several deer mounts were proudly displayed above the mirrors. Across the room were a coat rack, seating area for customers, and an assortment of large paintings hanging on the wall. Several brass spittoons were placed in the middle of the floor near the barber chairs.

Rose sat in the first chair near the door so he could watch people passing by and enjoy the sights and sounds of the beautiful autumn day. The sheriff introduced Rose to barber, Melges, and Mead and Olmstead took a seat and read the newspaper, while waiting for Rose.

"Well, Mr. Rose, what'll it be?" asked Melges.

"I'd like a close shave, hair trim, and moustache wax, if you don't mind. I'm getting my photo taken today and want to look my best."

"We'll get you fixed up and lookin' mighty fine. Sit back and relax."

Melges put the cape on Rose and sharpened the straight-edge razor on the leather strap that hung on the arm of the chair. Melges tilted back the chair and placed a warm towel on his face for a few minutes. Then with a soft bristled brush, he lathered the face and neck with warm shaving cream. Rose closed his eyes and felt the blade skillfully skim along his face.

"This is the best shave I've had in quite some time," said Rose.

"Thank you, sir, I aim to please," replied Melges.

After the shave, Melges trimmed the moustache and added wax to make the ends twirl up. The hair cut came last.

"Now, don't cut it short," instructed Rose.

"No, sir, I'll just give it a trim," replied Melges.

Finally, Melges was done. He twirled the chair around so Rose was facing the mirror.

"You did a fine job, Mr. Melges. I've never looked so good. Now, what do I owe ya?"

"Not a thing, it's on the house. I know you've got a tough road ahead of you tomorrow."

"Well, thank you, kindly, Mr. Melges. I do appreciate your hospitality."

Then the trio exited the barber shop and walked the short distance to N.B. Anderson's Studio, where Rose sat for his photo.

Mr. Anderson had quite a reputation as an artist and business man. He had another studio in Morton, which his wife managed. Anderson had an eye for color, shade and effect, and combined with first-class equipment, produced sharp negatives that brought out the best qualities of all his subjects.

Mr. Anderson greeted Rose at the door and escorted him to his studio which was at the rear of the building.

"Find yourself a comfortable seat and we'll get started," said Anderson. "What type of pose did you have in mind; portrait or profile?"

"Well, I thought portrait would be most appropriate. This will be the last photo I'll ever have taken and am doing this for my family," said Rose.

"I'll take a couple shots and let you decide; how's that?"

"That's fine by me," said Rose.

Anderson set up his equipment and made sure the lighting was just right before he pushed the shutter.

"Don't move now; I'll set up for another shot."

Rose sat patiently, while Anderson adjusted the lighting for the next pose. Through the lens, Rose appeared as a statue, not moving a muscle while Anderson focused the camera lens and took the next photo.

"Okay, I think we're done here. Both of these photos are excellent. Which would you prefer?"

"Well, a poor subject makes a good picture," commented Rose. "I can't decide which one would be best, so I'll take some of each."

"That's a good idea and you're family will cherish these photos forever. Anderson shook Rose's hand and said, "I wish you well, Mr. Rose, and pray Governor Merriam has a change of heart and commutes your sentence before tomorrow."

"Thank you, sir, you've been most kind but I'm ready to meet my fate."

After directing the sending of a dozen pictures to his father, along with the bill, he then proceeded to the undertaker's to select his own coffin at Bell & Person's on Mill Street. Such nerve as this in the face of what awaited him was perhaps never before demonstrated.

For over twenty years, Mr. Bell had lain young and old to rest with skill and kindly care, and was versed on all the latest developments of his profession. The first floor of this building was occupied as a furniture store and storeroom, and the upper floor, pertained to the undertaking business.

Mr. Bell met Rose at the front door, invited him upstairs, and walked him through the huge array of caskets that took up the entire second floor.

"What did you have in mind, Mr. Rose?" asked the undertaker.

"Well, it should be simple, but of a strong wood, since I'm going to be resting in it for a long time to come," replied Rose with a chuckle.

After quite some time, Rose finally chose a fine coffin made of burl wood with silver trim, and lined with gray satin. A plate included the inscription, "At Rest."

"I think this one will be perfect, Mr. Bell, and I'm sure I'll rest comfortably in it for all eternity," Rose laughed.

"You've made a wise choice, Mr. Rose. It's the best casket of the bunch and made of fine quality materials. I'll make sure all's in order and contact the family about funeral arrangements."

"Thank you kindly for your courteous assistance with this ugly matter. You've been most patient with me as I pick just the right box for my final resting place."

Mr. Bell gave Rose a hearty handshake and wished him well.

Rose and his escorts left the funeral parlor, walked back to the small jail where he entered his cell, and laid down on the bed for a short nap before supper.

When he awoke an hour later; it was already dark and very cold in the small, cramped cell.

He asked Sheriff Mead, "Could I get some heat in here and an extra blanket?"

"I'll see what I can do," replied the sheriff.

Mead was gone for quite awhile but finally returned with some blankets and some wood to start a fire in the small, potbellied stove in the corner of the jail. It wasn't long before the warmth from the wood burning stove gave Rose a feeling of comfort and peace.

He stepped over to the washbasin, splashed water on his face, and felt refreshed. Rose sat down at the small, wooden desk and wrote several letters. At 6 o'clock, the sheriff brought him a hearty supper of fried oysters. After supper, he finished writing letters, read from the Bible, and completed reading a "dime" novel.

Later he asked Mead, "How'd you like to play a few rounds of poker?"

"That'd be a fine way to pass the time. I'll get the cards."

Rose enjoyed the company; they played poker, swapped stories, told jokes and laughed for hours.

At about 10 o'clock, Mead said, "You about ready to call it a night? You're lookin' mighty tired."

"Not yet," replied Rose. "Since this is my last night on this earth, I'd like to stay awake a bit longer, if it's alright with you, sheriff?"

"That's fine by me, Rose. I'll sit with you as long as you'd like," and they played a few more rounds of poker.

It wasn't until about 10:30, when Rose finally bid the sheriff a goodnight. He put on his night clothes, said his prayers, slipped under the warm blankets, and slept, long and hard until 3:30 the following morning.

SCENES FROM ROSE'S FINAL TRIP
OCTOBER 15, 1891

Brown County Jail where Rose stayed for 3 years.
(Courtesy Brown County Historical Society Collection, New Ulm, MN)

New Ulm Depot, Rose left here early morning October 15th
(Courtesy Elroy Ubl's photo collection)

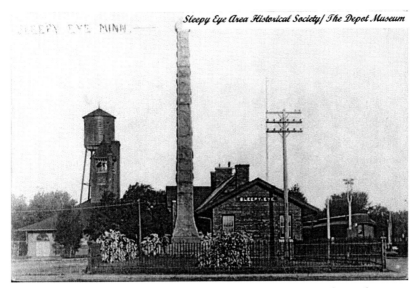

Arrived Sleepy Eye Depot and walked to Commercial Hotel

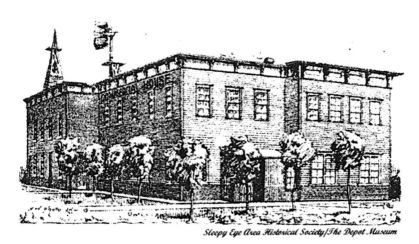

Rose ate last breakfast here, Commercial Hotel, Sleepy Eye
(Photos courtesy Sleepy Eye Area Historical Society)

Arrived Redwood Falls Depot and rode in omnibus to jail.

Rose got a shave in J. Melges Barber Shop at 3 o'clock.

(Photos courtesy Redwood County Historical Society)

N.B. Anderson and studio where Rose sat for photos

Undertaker H.N. Bell and Bell & Person's Furniture Store.
(Photos courtesy Redwood County Historical Society)

Redwood County Courthouse 1893
(Photo courtesy Redwood County Historical Society)

CHAPTER EIGHTEEN
Last Letter

The following is Rose's last letter to his parents, written on October 15, 1891, the night before his execution, and included in *Redwood Gazette*, October 22, 1891:

Dearest Ones at Home: It is with a sad heart that I pen these last few lines, realizing that the time is drawing near when I will be launched into eternity.

The thought of those that are dearer to me than life are my only regret, but the hope of the future sustains me. You cannot realize the feeling I have.

Oh God, if I could only prove to the world my innocence, what would I give. Ah, willingly would I lie down my life, dear though it may be, were it 10,000 times dearer to me than it is. Yes, would I gladly do it to wipe the terrible stigma from the path of my poor heartbroken parents.

But we have a blessed truth that whosoever believeth on Him shall have everlasting life. In Him, and Him only, do I place my trust.

I am reconciled to my fate, and ask God's blessing to rest upon you all, and assist you in bearing the burden of your grief, and hope and trust that when the great reaper gathereth his harvest, I will meet you all in that bright home of love.

I had my picture taken today, and N.B. Anderson will send you one dozen, and I want to send one to the following address, John C. Geiger, New Ulm, Minn., as I promised him one. One also to this address, if she wishes it: Miss Alma, New Ulm, Minn. I wish also to enclose a letter to her with this last request.

Bidding all good-bye and asking you all to bear your trials bravely as you may believe I shall, again I will say good-bye, and God bless you all.

From your affectionate son and brother, William Rose.[1]

CHAPTER NINETEEN
Death March

Rose slept five hours and was called at 3:30 a.m. on October 16, on as beautiful a fall morning as was ever known. The sky was clear of any trace of a cloud. The full moon had swung down toward the western horizon to throw long shadows on everything outside, while the light of day was fast approaching.

As soon as Rose was up, he stepped into his black suit and shirt of darkest blue. He was perfectly cool and collected, and asked the sheriff for breakfast. It was slow in coming and while he waited, Reverend Sinclair appeared, only on account of Rose's earnest request to accompany him to the gallows.

Rose spoke freely with the reverend and remarked, "This is the happiest night that I ever passed in my life. There was only one thing to mar my happiness -- thoughts of my mother. If I only knew, if I could realize that my mother was reconciled, I would die the happiest man upon earth."[1]

For the first time during three long years of confinement, the strong man broke down, and tears coursed over his pale, sallow cheeks as he spoke so tenderly and lovingly of his dear mother. Then he recovered his composure, paced restlessly up and down once or twice, and sat down to his breakfast of eggs and fried oysters, eating heartily. Mr. Sinclair then read from the Scriptures and prayed with the condemned man.

"Now the end is very near, Rose," said the reverend, "and I want you to tell me in whom and what you trust."

Rose said, "I trust only in Him who died for me."

Rose lit a cigar and puffed vigorously for some five minutes. Then he called to the sheriff outside.

"You can come in when you like. I am ready," declared Rose.

Mr. Sinclair asked Rose if there was any last request or message he would like to give.

"The only request I have," said Rose gravely and courteously, "is that you follow my corpse to the grave."₂

The sheriff then entered with Deputies Olmstead and McClintock, Sheriff Billings of Otter Tail County, and ex-sheriff Schmid of Brown County, and produced the dreaded warrant of death.

Rose said, "You don't need to read it, unless it is required."

"It is the law," replied Sheriff Mead, and Rose listened attentively to the reading.₃ Then he was told that friends outside wished to see him.

"I would like to see them all," Rose said, and three New Ulm gentlemen were admitted. He shook hands with each, and told them that he would die an innocent man. Then, without waiting for the word, he crossed his hands behind his back and turned them toward the sheriff to be handcuffed, but a few seconds later, he requested the manacles be removed in order to get some trinkets and money out of his pocket. These trifles he handed to Deputy Olmstead to be given to the undertaker.

The noble bearing of the condemned murderer touched every heart. He seemed to offer himself freely, almost as a sacrifice. Knowing the certain fate in store for him, he met it with heroic courage.

At 4:50 a.m. the death march to the gallows began. Deputies Olmstead and McClintock led the way, and then came the condemned man, followed by Sheriff Mead and Reverend Sinclair bringing up the rear. They left the little cell known as the jail, crossed a narrow hallway, and walked reverently into the enclosure of death.

Twenty-two steep steps, broken by a narrow landing, led to the platform. Rose mounted them firmly, without assistance, and placed himself upon the trap, glancing downward to see that he had made no mistake.₄

Rose was a very handsome-looking gentleman. His face looked marble-white against the jet-black hair and moustache. He stood over six feet tall. He looked like an athlete, very well-proportioned, and with a magnificent girth of chest. He weighed 190 pounds. His head was covered with closely cut black hair, and was well-shaped. His forehead, naturally high, was made doubly so by premature baldness. He wore a heavy black moustache, rather closely trimmed in front, but to the ends had been given a coquettish twirl. For half an inch down either cheek, sideburns were blocked out. His eyebrows were black and very heavy. His long eyelashes drooped over eyes of dead brown, which looked at every spectator straight and fair. This man, soon to be strangled, could have passed in any metropolis as a "Beau Brummel."₅

Usually, upon the face of the condemned, there steals, as the hour of death approaches nearer and nearer, a pallor never to be mistaken, once it is seen. It tells not only of death, but of horror unutterable. No trace of this was seen upon the almost classic face of Rose.

CHAPTER TWENTY
The Hanging

The hanging occurred in a rough frame structure, unpainted, and just to the rear of the snug, little frame house called a jail. Its dimensions were 18 x 20 feet, and it had been built about 1890. The pine structure, with its suggestion of death and doom, was not pleasant to look upon.

The gallows had originally been built for the execution of John Lee, at Alexandria, and afterwards used for the execution of the Barretts. It was then put in place at Redwood, and remained standing ever since.

Once, it had been ready for the execution of Clifton Holden, but at the eleventh hour, Governor Merriam commuted his death sentence.

Nearly everybody looked for similar action on the part of Governor Merriam in the Rose case. All day the streets had echoed with complaints of executive clemency in one case (the Holden case), and want of it where it was really deserved (the Rose case).

If ever injustice was done, all admitted, it was in these two murder cases in Redwood County. This fact impressed itself upon everybody and added to the dramatic intensity of the scene.[1]

The frame building enclosing the scaffold was lighted with kerosene lamps, long-wicked, making everything look a sickly yellow. In front of the scaffold was a line of men, presumably favorites of the sheriff, and armed, for excuse, with old muskets resurrected from some vault.

Sheriff Mead invited Sheriff DeFrate of Douglas County, and Sheriff Billings of Otter Tail County, who was set to hang Goheen at Fergus Falls on October 23. Other favorites of the sheriff were present, among them H.G. Hayes, editor of the *Sleepy Eye Herald*. Of course, this wasn't in violation of the law as it was interpreted in Redwood.

And that the majesty of justice might not be further violated, there was placed a cordon of burlesque comedians all about the jail. These men, mostly old residents of Redwood, were likewise armed with muskets, having bayonets about a yard long. It seemed the duty of these old-timers, armed with their brief authority, to keep legitimate newspaper men and strangers away, while those who were known were let past the line to put eager eyes to the many knotholes and cracks in the shambles, where they had an excellent view of the hanging.

Several drunken men were allowed to congregate on the west side of the structure, and a big free fight was prevented only by the appearance of Rose upon the scaffold. As it was, Rose must have plainly heard the profane wrangling as he mounted the twenty-two steps leading him to his death.[2]

At Rose's request, Reverend Sinclair offered the final prayer from the scaffold. In a few low, but deeply touching words, he commended the spirit of Rose to his Maker. Rose then glanced at the little crowd of people below with his piercing dark eyes, and firmly, as if weighing every word, as if he would bring home to everyone his truth, as if he spoke in the very presence of God -- he said his last words:

Gentlemen, you realize that I stand on this platform tonight as a poor, unfortunate man, who in a few minutes must swing. I see a number of faces before me which I know, and some of you, gentlemen, will surely live to see the day that I shall be declared innocent. It is not by the strong arm of God that this is done, but by the strong arm of the law. I must bow to it.

Gentlemen, I believe, and I know, that the man who killed Lufkin was Eli Slover. I repeat it, gentlemen, that Slover is the guilty man.

Watch that old man, Slover, and see whether my words don't come true.

I thank you for being here and for the kindnesses I have received from you. Gentlemen, I bid you good-bye.[3]

"Sheriff, do your duty," Rose quietly remarked as his last words died away.

Sheriff Mead, into whose hands fell the dreadful task of execution, at last appeared. Rose stood stoically upon the trap door, and while he was being pinioned, he remarked to Deputy Olmstead, "It takes a good lot of nerve to do this."

Olmstead replied, "You have a good lot of nerve."

"No more than an innocent man should have," said Rose.[4]

Then, as the rope was placed about his neck, he said, in tones of unutterable regret, as he glanced up at the hemp strands.

"Boys, this looks pretty tough."

Sheriff Mead quickly adjusted the noose, and just as the black cap of knitted goods, tailored by H.P. Nelson, was drawn down over the handsome face, Rose exclaimed, "Goodbye all."[5]

These were the last words Rose uttered. There was an instant when all hearts stopped.

Then Sheriff Mead, his face ghastly white, placed his hand on the big lever.

Reverend Sinclair had meant to offer a final invocation, but before the first word was uttered, the sheriff pulled the lever by his side -- it was 5 o'clock sharp.

The trap fell with a crash and there was a jar that shook the entire structure, a spasmodic upward movement of the pinioned legs, a fierce clasp of the manacled hands, and a loud snap; the body of William Rose lay in a heap upon the floor, the noose tight about his neck, and three feet or more of the rope stretching along his side. The rope had broken, cut into by the hook in the beam above. Imperfectly tested, the rope had snapped in two.

The horror-stricken spectators stood absolutely without movement, as if carved out of granite. Sheriff Mead was the one to break the spell.

"Get him up! Get him up!" the sheriff said in a hoarse whisper.

Deputy Olmsted, who had stood to the right of the prisoner, jumped down through the trap. Another deputy and Coroner Pease raised the body and carried it up the steps, where it was laid, full-length, face upwards, upon the readjusted trap.

It took but a minute to carry him back to the gallows, and not a word was spoken by anyone. It was an appalling scene as the trap was raised, and the second noose, dangling above, was pulled down and placed about the neck.

Then the trap was sprung again without any attempt to raise Rose to his feet, and the body slipped slowly downward and hung suspended. The body raised itself convulsively a time or two, and a shudder passed over his frame as Rose's spirit finally escaped into eternity.

It must have been a slow, agonizing death, as the heart continued to beat for six and a half minutes, and a trace of it was still felt for five minutes longer.

At the end of twenty-three minutes, a stroke of the knife lowered his body to the ground. When the cap was removed, the face was serene, as if in sleep. There was profuse hemorrhaging from the nostrils, however. Frightfully disfigured as it was, the neck was not cut. [6]

The Rose supporters who witnessed the execution believed that when the rope broke, this was a definite sign from God that Rose was innocent of the crime. And in Rose's final days, he had declared to all those who testified against him, "Vengeance is the Lord's; God have mercy on their souls. Grieve not for those who plot against me; for they receive what they deserve." [7]

THE GALLOWS.

(Sketch, Minneapolis Tribune, October 16, 1891)

Coroner Pease viewed the remains, and pronounced Rose dead. The end of the dangling noose was removed from the neck and thrown aside. The body was taken in charge by Undertaker, J.W. Wardell of Tracy, and enclosed in the silver-trimmed, burl wood burial coffin. The undertaker acted under the direction of Rose's mother, and at noon the body, accompanied by Reverend Sinclair, was taken to Tracy.

Rose's body was conveyed to Tracy by the midday train on Friday. At all the stations along the way, small groups of people were standing and a great run was made on the daily papers. When the train bearing

Rose's remains arrived in Tracy, it was surrounded by about 200 people attracted through curiosity.

Mrs. Rose was on the platform at Tracy when the train arrived. When the coffin was taken out of the car, she displayed great emotion, and had to be supported by Reverend Sinclair. Mrs. Rose was in great distress. Reverend Sinclair gave her his arm, and led her to a buggy that awaited her. Levi Montgomery, a relative, and the reverend seated themselves next to her for the three-mile drive to the Rose farm. There was a wagon, containing the coffin and driven by a hired hand, which went before the buggy.

Upon their arrival at the farm, the casket was taken into the house, where the family wished to see the face of the dead man, which was still and peaceful as if in sleep. One of the sisters fainted when she saw the face of Rose, and had to be carried into another room.[8]

Reverend Sinclair then told the family all about the last hours with Rose.

Sinclair said, "From my first contact with him, he declared firmly his innocence, and held to the very last. He often said, 'God, who knows the heart, knows that I am innocent, and He will stand by me when I die.' Several times we had talks about the meaning of Christ's work. He understood fully its full meaning and professed without doubting his saving interest in Christ's future redemption of the soul. Almost the last word he said to me was to give me this assurance of his hope in Christ."[9]

Sinclair conveyed these thoughts to Rose's mother about his final days, conducted worship and prayed with the family. He left with Levi Montgomery at 11 o'clock that night. Reverend Sinclair was requested to remain for the funeral the following day, but could not, on account of other engagements.

CHAPTER TWENTY-ONE

The Funeral

The funeral of William Rose was held Sunday afternoon, October 18, at the home of his parents, four miles south of Tracy, with internment at the Tracy Cemetery. The services were conducted by Reverend Terwilliger of Fulda, at the request of the family.

An immense crowd was in attendance that cold, gloomy day. They anticipated something sensational in the discourse, and that the preacher would express some opinion as to the guilt or innocence of the deceased. In this, they were disappointed, as no reference was made to this subject.

After the funeral, the casket was loaded onto the buggy, followed by over one hundred teams, along with many friends and neighbors, who escorted Rose to his final resting place. As the family gathered around the grave, Martha Rose, with tears streaming down her face, placed a bouquet of red roses on her son's coffin. Roses were William's favorite flower.

After everyone gathered at the gravesite, the reverend read a few scriptures from the Bible and ended with a reading of the 23rd Psalm, along with a prayer. This was followed by a male quartet from Tracy who furnished the music, and ended by singing "Amazing Grace," Rose's favorite hymn. There was not a dry eye among the crowd, and mourners were slow to leave the scene.

Many of those in attendance were shocked to see old man Slover at the cemetery. Rose supporters were up in arms at the sight of a man who knowingly sent an innocent man to the gallows and they were ready to physically remove him from the cemetery when someone hollered out,

"Slover's got a right to pay his respects to this poor, wretched man, and nobody better say nothin' different about it."

By this time, most of the mourners were slowly getting into their buggies as a gentle rain began to fall. But a few men lingered, one of them being Rose's close friend, John Averill, who wept long and hard; his tears falling along with the rain onto Rose's coffin.

Another man who lingered alone in the shadows was ol' man Slover, who quietly walked up alongside Averill. John finally looked over at the old man and saw tears streaming down his sunken cheeks.

Slover then proclaimed to those still standing at the gravesite, "Gentlemen, this is awful."

"It certainly is," replied John. "Are you sure you've got the right man?"

Slover replied, "I don't know, John, but I hope so."[1]

John -- and all others hearing this remark -- were appalled, and immediately left Slover standing at the gravesite all by himself. They were horrified to hear Slover admit that he was unsure of his conviction against Rose, but hoped he'd done the right thing.

It was a very somber day as Rose was finally laid to rest on a cold, dreary day in October 1891.

CHAPTER TWENTY-TWO

The Aftermath

Rose's execution was repulsively shocking, and as cruel an exhibition as was ever offered upon the scaffold. The extremely tragic ending of the life of William Rose, strangled to death in a bungling manner in a building no better than a shed, was generally looked upon in southwestern Minnesota as a deliberate judicial murder.

It was a horrible affair throughout the execution. It appeared that an imperfectly tested rope broke and dropped the unconscious man to the floor. And there seemed no good reason why the dying man should not have been lifted to his feet when brought up the second time.

Rose suffered a slow, agonizing death by strangulation, and the scene was more like a "hog killing" than an execution. Rose's neck was not lacerated by the rope, and his face, unmarred by any sign of strangulation, was as peaceful in death as in sleep, showing that death was painless. One can only hope that this noble and courageous man, who suffered so much pain and torment in his short life, died peacefully, and was now at rest with his Maker.[1]

After the execution, many stories circulated with regard to the hanging. One was that when the trap was sprung the first time, the guards, fearful that Rose might come to, sprang upon his prostrate body and attempted to strangle him. Another was that in the fall, one of his arms and left leg were broken. And another was that Rose said, as he was being carried back to the scaffold the second time, "Go on with the hanging, I am innocent."[2]

All these stories were nonsense -- all lies, manufactured by young reporters trying to make a name for themselves. True, the rope broke, but Rose was as dead when he struck the ground as he now is. Only because it was necessary to carry out the letter of the law was he hanged the second time. It was not due to any imperfect testing of the rope, nor was it any fault of Sheriff Mead's.

No man could have been more conscientious in the stern discharge of his duty than was the sheriff. Charlie Mead was the last man who would revel in the blood-curdling scenes of an execution. And yet, when standing face to face with his stern duty, he performed it manfully and courageously, and carried out the mandates of an outraged law, with a calm and unflinching determination that showed the stuff he was made of. One would never find a more courteous official or a truer man than Sheriff Mead. A politician he was not, but everyone agreed, he was an excellent sheriff.

Mead was known as a prosperous farmer residing in the western part of the county. The Republican county convention tendered him the nomination of sheriff in 1886. He accepted it and was elected with a good majority over his competitors. He had consistently been re-elected without opposition.

In appearance, Sheriff Mead was medium in stature, and appeared to have great endurance. He dressed plainly, and wore a slouch hat in all seasons, except winter, when he wore a heavy fur cap. He was warm-hearted, sympathetic, and generous, almost to a fault. "Charlie," as the boys called him, would share his last loaf of bread with anyone in need.

From the beginning of this case, Mead had hoped he would not be called on to carry out the stern mandate of the law upon Rose. Since Mead had never hanged a man, he and Deputy Sheriff McClintock spent some time in Minneapolis visiting with Sheriff Ege of Hennepin County, who had experience with the execution process. Mead wanted to make sure he carried out everything precisely and that no mistakes would be made.

When the case was finally decided, Mead faced the situation, and

performed his terrible duty calmly and unflinchingly, although his heart
was bleeding for poor Rose, whom he launched into eternity.[3]

Comments from citizens about Rose's execution appeared in the
Redwood Gazette on October 22, 1891, and are as follows:

*Reverend W.S. Vail, a local minister, stated the following in a sermon
after Rose's execution: In our opinion, the only justification for taking human life under any circumstances is self defense, and this right
must sometimes be exerted by the state, as well as, by individuals. If
it can be proven that capital punishment prevents murder in a much
greater degree than imprisonment, then to our mind the present law
is justified. But revenge or extermination is not an argument to be
tolerated for a moment. The strong arm of the law was not merely
raised against William Rose, but it served notice to every person of
murderous instincts throughout the state, that the state is bound to
protect the lives of its citizens from assassination, even to the extreme
limit of taking the life of the assassin.*[4]

*Honorable George T. Barr, state senator from Mankato commented:
I have never favored the 'death penalty' and would probably support
any reasonable measure looking to its abolishment. While the law
remains, however, it ought to be executed and the sentence having
once been imposed should, save in very rare cases, be carried out,
first, because it is the law, and again, because otherwise it soon fails
to have any effect in restraining crime.*[5]

*Ignatius Donnelly, Lieutenant Governor of Minnesota wrote: If the
Legislature should abolish capital punishment, the law should be so
changed as to take out of the hands of the governor the pardoning
power, in capital cases, so that the sentence of imprisonment for life
should mean all that its name implies. There should be a provision,
that in case of after-discovered testimony, the Supreme Court of the*

state should have the right to review the case and set the prisoner free, if, in their judgment, the testimony justified it.[6]

Ex-Governor A.R. McGill stated: Whether the crime of murder is minimized by punishing the murderer with death is still a much discussed question. If such punishment does not operate to deter the crime, then capital punishment is not justified. Whatever the power of the state, it has no right to take the life of a human being simply for revenge.[7]

An anonymous subscriber wrote: When so many circumstances point to a man's guilt as did to William Rose, it is almost incumbent upon him to prove his innocence. William Rose had nearly three years to clear himself, but instead of time tending to clear him of the crime, it tended to prove his guilt. He had three trials and the more he was tried the worse the case appeared. What of it if he was not hanged with the utmost neatness and dispatch? The bungling way in which he was removed will partly atone for the manner in which Lufkin was murdered.[8]

CHAPTER TWENTY-THREE
Slover's Statement

Rose died leaving a terrible charge upon Slover, and he being the only direct witness against Rose, it was well that the people of the community should follow the dying man's wishes and "watch Slover." If Slover were innocent, he could bear up under the false charge, but if he were really guilty, as Rose stated, then it was only a question of time before he would break down under the accusation. At the time, Slover expressed a willingness to be watched.[1]

That a man on the scaffold with his dying words should charge a well-known, respectable citizen with the crime of murder was sensational in the highest degree, but Mr. Slover made a statement that was of general interest at the time, because it not only showed the impossibility of the charge, but it explained away the charge that Lufkin had a large amount of money, and showed what had become of the money he had.

Rose charged that Lufkin had some $3500 just before he was killed, and that this money had never been accounted for. In an interview, Mr. Slover made the following statement about Lufkin's financial matters:

I can tell you all I know about Lufkin's money, stated Mr. Slover.

In April or May, before the murder, Mr. Lufkin traded a quarter section of land in Shetek Township, Murray County, for the northeast quarter of Section 22, in this town, receiving $600 "boot" in the trade, in cash and paper -- I think about half cash. There was a small mortgage on the land which he sold.

Mr. Lufkin owned another quarter section in Murray County, upon which he had borrowed $500 and given a mortgage. Part of this money was probably used for the expenses in the trials at the spring term of court in Murray County, when the Rose faction was before the grand jury with an accusation against Lufkin of incest, while Lufkin had the Roses examined for trying to blow up his house. Both charges were dropped by the grand jury, but Mr. Lufkin had the Roses hauled up for trial at the fall term for slander.

Lufkin had certificates of deposit for $400 in Jessup's Bank at Tracy when he was killed, which I suppose he had reserved for expenses at the upcoming trial. That $400 was paid out to Lufkin's daughters, Minnie and Grace, when the estate was settled.

As to that $1500 pension money Rose tells about, not one cent of it was paid out by the government. The pension -- which was $1030, instead of $1500 -- was granted on a claim for increase, with arrears. All that remained for Lufkin to do to get the money, as I afterwards heard from lawyer, Main, of Tracy, was to sign the vouchers and make the usual acknowledgments. Lufkin was intending to do this at the time he was shot. So the government never paid the money, though Congressman Lind afterwards proposed to try and get a special act of Congress passed so that the Lufkin girls could draw the money, which the murder prevented being paid, after it was allowed. ₂

Mr. Slover added that the facts about the money and the pension could be easily established by Banker Jessup and Commander Gibbs, of the G.A.R. post at Tracy.

Lufkin's two daughters, knew all about their father's money affairs, and they were not only pleased with Mr. Slover's relation to them, but had asked him to make out a bill for his trouble on their account after the tragedy, as well as, for their father's board, which Mr. Slover declined to do.

CHAPTER TWENTY-FOUR
Was a Confession Made?

There was a report in January 1900, that Eli Slover had made a confession that he, and not William Rose, was guilty of the crime of murdering Moses Lufkin at the Slover residence on the evening of August 22, 1888.

The only foundation for the report was a telegram heard going over the wires along the south side of the county that Eli Slover had been informed by his physician in California that he could not live but a few days longer, and that Slover then made a confession of having committed the crime before he passed away.[1]

But the reports of the death and deathbed confession of Eli Slover, which came by way of Lamberton and Vesta, were myths -- nothing but rumors -- and there was no truth in them whatsoever.

On January 22, a letter was received from a member of the family at Salem, Oregon, where the members were residing, that the entire family was in good health, and enjoying the climate, etc., of that country very much.

The sons and other relatives of the family, residing in Gales Township, confirmed this fact and said that their father would never have any confession to make, except that the right man suffered the penalty for the murder of Moses Lufkin.

The *Tracy Republican* had the following: "Time and again has some cute individual started the story that Will Rose was innocent." This time it was a report from Redwood Falls that had been published in all the Twin City dailies that "Slover confessed on his deathbed that he was the one who took Lufkin's life."[2]

The article in question had too many earmarks of untruth to catch people who were conversant with the facts.

"In the first place, Slover lived in Oregon, not California, and secondly, instead of making a confession on his deathbed, which happened some days ago according to the story, Slover was as well and happy as usual or was on the 17th of this month, as reported in a letter from his daughter to a lady friend in Tracy."[3]

They say the story may have been perpetrated by Julius Schmahl, the prominent editor of the *Redwood Gazette,* and there probably was no foundation whatsoever for it. Schmahl later served several terms in two state offices: Secretary of State and State Treasurer. He always maintained that Rose was innocent.

CHAPTER TWENTY-FIVE

Other Possible Suspects

If guilty, Rose's actions at the last were such as to place him among the most hardened criminals the world has ever known. If innocent, he went to his death with the heroism of a martyr of old. And, whether innocent or guilty, he met his death like a noble man.

It has now been over 120 years since this terrible crime, and still one wonders if an innocent man was condemned to hang for another's dastardly deed.

Truth be told, Moses Lufkin was a most despicable and lecherous man, and by his own admission, believed he would die a violent death. So this would bring one to ponder other suspects motivated in committing this heinous crime.

The first possible suspect, and the one Rose accused of the crime, would be Eli Slover, his motive being the money. Moses lived with Eli for several months before the shooting. Slover was quite familiar with all of Moses' recent financial transactions and probably wanted to get his hands on Lufkin's cash, as Eli had lots of debtors hounding him. The $1500 in cash was never accounted for, and there was no evidence ever shown that Rose had secured it.

Slover could have easily plotted the murder, shot Lufkin himself, and instructed his family to tell the same story when authorities arrived on the scene. Eli knew of the feud between the Lufkins and the Roses, and William made an easy scapegoat.

At the time of the murder, Eli admitted to having three guns in his house -- with one always loaded. Moses also had a revolver and always carried it with him, but the revolver was never located after the murder.

What became of it? Did someone in the Slover family use it to commit the crime?

Another possible suspect within the Slover family could be Eli's eldest daughter, Angie, who was purported to have been in a bedroom at the time of the murder -- but was she really? Could it be that while Lufkin lived with the Slovers, he made inappropriate advances toward Angie, and she, being humiliated and ashamed, found Lufkin's revolver, crept out of the bedroom window to where Moses was lounging that night, shot him, and disposed of Lufkin's gun later, her motive, that of revenge? Angie, being distraught over a lecherous, old man's unwanted advances on her young, innocent body, may have come across his revolver one day and later plotted to kill him whenever she had the chance.

It was reported in the "personal section" of the *Redwood Gazette* on October 29, 1891 that "Miss Angie Slover arrived home on October 14, having been in the eastern part of the state the past nine months."[1] One can only wonder why Angie was away from her family for nine months, returning home two days before Rose's execution. Angie could have been a very probable suspect, but was never interrogated by the authorities, who believed she was too young at the time to handle a revolver, and who were acting, based on Slover's testimony, stating she was in the bedroom at the time of the shooting.

Then there is the suspect Barney Benjamin, the son-in-law Lufkin threatened with a revolver one night, reminding him that he would shoot him if he ever saw him again. It would be quite possible that Barney sought revenge for this vicious threat and banishment from Lufkin's home where he once lived with his beautiful wife, Grace. At the time of the murder, nobody was sure of Barney's whereabouts. It could have been that Barney was living in the area and plotted to get rid of Moses so he could be with Grace again.

What about the daughter, Minnie, who at one time borrowed $5.00 from Wes Averill to purchase a revolver in order to protect herself from her father, and threatened him with it on several occasions? The many years Minnie endured Lufkin's incestuous attacks were probably more than she could bear, and another justifiable motive for homicide. But it had been reported in a local newspaper that Minnie was in Iowa visiting with her sister, Grace, at the time of the murder.

There are probably many more suspects, and one can only speculate on circumstances and motives, but it seems so ironic that Moses Lufkin, a man despised by many -- an eccentric man with a violent temper, who committed rape and incest, who was involved in illegal activities, and who had financial difficulties -- was never convicted of any crime and never spent a day in jail.

But William Rose -- a fairly respectable, God-fearing man, whose only misfortune was to fall in love with Lufkin's beautiful daughter, Grace -- was convicted of murder on purely circumstantial evidence, and his short life ended at the gallows --- hanged not once, but twice. One can only surmise what a huge miscarriage of justice has taken place.

CHAPTER TWENTY-SIX
The Fate of those Left Behind

The Rose execution left a lasting impression, not only on those who witnessed it, but also on those who lived in this county and state. It was an historic event that would be recorded for all time.

But life goes on, and after a time "the execution" was not a constant topic of discussion in Redwood County. Some of those who had been involved with the Rose case met untimely deaths, as evidenced below.

It was commonly known by residents of the community that Judge Webber was never wholly convinced of Rose's guilt. The failure of the State to show what had become of $1500 that Lufkin received from the sale of his farm shortly before he took up residence with the Slover family was the strongest evidence that the crime had been committed for money, and Rose had a right to use it that way. In fact, the evidence of the State was that Rose had never been in Slover's house before the murder, and the $1500 in cash was never accounted for, so what became of it?

Benjamin Webber was elected Judge of the Ninth Judicial District and assumed office in January 1883. He first presided over a Redwood County term of court at Redwood Falls, convening June 5 of that year. He continued as judge until October 1906, when he resigned. The events following his resignation were quite tragic.[1]

Although his wealth was estimated at $100,000, fear of the poorhouse drove the judge to take his life. Judge Webber had been downcast ever since he resigned his judgeship, and intimated frequently to friends that he would be better off dead. The loss of his salary as judge, together with his wife's continued illness and mounting medical bills, weighed heavily upon him. Still, his friends did not believe he would contemplate suicide.

The judge had brooded more than usual over his misfortunes, and one morning he rose earlier than his custom, and, after awakening the servant girl, left the house.

The maid prepared breakfast for Mr. Webber, but as hours passed and he did not appear, she became alarmed. She notified the police, who immediately came out to the residence, and found the judge hanging from a rafter in his barn.

The judge had mounted a box, wrapped a harness strap around his neck, buckled the other end over a stringer, and jumped off. He had been dead for several hours before he was found.

Judge Webber was to have been the guest of honor at a banquet that week, tendered him by the Brown County Bar Association in honor of his long service on the bench, from which he had resigned only a few weeks before.

Judge Webber was considered one of the most brilliant men at the Minnesota Bar. He served nearly 24 years on the bench, and his decisions were rarely reversed by the Supreme Court. He was 74 years old when he died.[2]

Judge Benjamin Webber
(Courtesy Brown County Historical Society Collection, New Ulm, MN)

The prosecution attorney, Michael Madigan, took office as county attorney of Redwood County in January 1887, and was the prosecutor in the convictions of the three murderers of 1888: John Gorres, Clifton Holden, and William Rose -- a record no other county attorney approached.

Madigan labored tirelessly on these three cases and used alcohol heavily at this time. Madigan's rigorous court schedules and high-profile cases kept him from his family much of the time, and this left his wife,

Nettie, alone to care for four small children.

In August and September 1888, Nettie took comfort in the arms of another, and by November of that year, they divorced. Madigan was awarded custody of the four children: Alfred, 7; David, 6; Samuel, 4; and Francis, 2 years of age.

During Madigan's prosecution of the Rose case, he became very bitter when Rose was acquitted in the first trial, and again in the second trial. By the third trial, Madigan wanted Rose's conviction and stopped at nothing to get it. Madigan was suspected of meeting with certain witnesses prior to their testimony -- coaxing them, and possibly even bribing them to give the testimony he wanted in order to bring in a conviction against Rose.

But Madigan himself came afoul of the law on April 5, 1893 when he was charged with perjury, found guilty, and sentenced to three years and three months at Stillwater State Prison.

After he served his sentence, Madigan returned to Redwood Falls and renewed his law practice. Madigan had been humiliated and felt an injustice had been served. He took action to have his conviction set aside, but Judge Webber denied the move, and Madigan appealed to the State Supreme Court.

Madigan not only lost his case, but was disbarred from practicing law in Minnesota. He eventually married Mattie Murphy from Kirkwood, Ohio and they had three children. Madigan and his family moved to Seattle in 1898, where he was accepted by the bar association there. Madigan's busy law practice, alcoholism, and his own personal problems led to an early death at the age of 49 on June 10, 1900 in Seattle, Washington.[3]

Michael Morris Madigan - Born Sept. 10, 1851 Died June 10, 1900

Michael Madigan
(Courtesy Lucile Madigan Kinzel, Daughter of Michael & Mattie)

The defense attorney, William Erwin, attended law school in Albany, New York and was admitted to the bar in May 1881. As a lawyer, Erwin had a remarkable career, especially in criminal defense. He appeared for the defense in more than a hundred homicide cases, many of which were of national notoriety. His sympathies always championed the cause of the weak and oppressed. In the courtroom, his conduct was always that of a soldier in the battle for the right, with no thought but for victory.

While practicing in the St. Paul area, he was given the name, "The Pine Tree of the North." Tall and stately like a soldier, the name seemed fitting. The strength of his mind was as powerful as the grasp of his hand, and his charitable nature was made boundless by the scope of his imagination.

Erwin and his wife eventually moved to Miami and were there for five years. They moved from Minnesota due to Mrs. Erwin's health, as she was convalescing from typhoid fever, and after a short time, they decided to make Miami their permanent home. Erwin suffered two long years with a malignant cancer and died at his home at the age of 65.₄

William Wallis Erwin
(From obit, The Miami Metropolis, September 14, 1908)

John Rose, William's brother and the family's second-eldest son, worked for the railroad as an engine hostler. On November 10, 1896, he was fatally injured at the Illinois Central Railroad coal yard, near the roundhouse.

It seems John Rose and John O'Brien were at work on Engine 9 around 10:00 a.m. and had just coaled up. Rose was standing on the toolbox between the cab of the engine and the heavy oak chute, which is let down from the coal bins above. At some point, a piece of coal caught in the hinge and prevented the chute from going to its proper place. Mr. O'Brien supposed the chute was caught and started the engine back. Mr. Rose was in the act of pulling the chute down again to push it up properly when the moving engine caught his body between the corner of the cab and the chute he was handling.

His cries attracted the attention of his helper; the engine was stopped almost immediately and started ahead to loosen the pinioned man. Mr. Rose fell on the toolbox and his companion caught him, preventing him from going over the side of the tender. His body appeared quite limp and helpless as he was moved away from the cab. The wounded man was carried to the roundhouse and a physician and the patrol wagon summoned. There were no bad outward marks upon his body, but he seemed to be hurt internally, and complained of his back. He was taken to his home on a stretcher and carefully examined. It was found that he was badly crushed internally through the region of the abdomen. The lower part of the body was paralyzed and he did not recover from the terrible shock, though he was conscious and talked about it. He was in great pain after the accident, and his pulse did not regain strength. His condition was critical and he died at 2:30 that afternoon. John Rose was 34 years old and left a wife and two small children.[5]

What happened to Grace Lufkin was a terrible tragedy. She had a very difficult and unhappy childhood, and despised her father for putting an end to her romance with Will. During the third trial, Erwin brought to light Lufkin's possible intimate relations with Grace, as well as, with his niece, Alice Sloan.

One newspaper account reported that Grace was present with two other ladies at Mr. Slover's residence the night of the shooting. Instead of being in Iowa, it may have been possible that Grace secretly returned to the area to visit her father. Hatred boiled within her, knowing she'd committed perjury at the incest trial to help clear her father of any incest allegations. It's quite possible Lufkin forced himself upon Grace during the time Alice Sloan lived with them, or possibly on other occasions. Grace wanted revenge. She had a gun and could have secretly plotted a murder with Eli Slover as her accomplice. It seems quite likely that someone in the Slover household conveniently seated Lufkin with his back exposed near the open window that night, making an easy target for the shooter.

After Grace's failed marriage to Barney Benjamin, and testifying at her father's incest trial, she left the area, spending some time in Iowa as a teacher, and finally moving in with her sister, Minnie, in Chicago. At some point, while living with her sister, Grace became deeply despondent and was suffering from temporary mental aberration over the course that the Lufkin family history was pursuing. She was found in her bedroom one morning in early May 1890. She had committed suicide by cutting her throat with a razor. She was only 27 years old, and is presumed to be buried in an unmarked grave somewhere in Chicago. Grace went to the grave fulfilling her promise to Will -- they'd be together one day -- if not in this life, then in the next.[6]

And then there's Eli Slover. What if rumors of a deathbed confession were true? Slover suffered from an extended illness, and at one point may have been at death's door. To clear his conscience, he might have confessed to his family that he was the one who murdered Lufkin, his motive being the money. If Eli did indeed murder Lufkin, then he may have suffered a fate worse than death. Imagine the long years of harboring the terrible secret of being the person responsible for sending an innocent man to the gallows. Slover passed away in Corning, California. He was 95 years of age.[7]

A most disastrous fire occurred in Tracy about a month after Rose's funeral, and for a time it appeared that nearly the whole town north of the railroad was doomed to destruction.

The fire was first discovered just before 11 o'clock while people were comfortably seated in church, and before the alarm was sounded, the flames were well underway. The fire started either under the sidewalk in front of the old post office and Hughes' building, or from the basement of the buildings. It ran along the sills of the buildings, getting a good head start before showing above the sidewalk, and when seen, was reaching up to the windowsills of two or three buildings.

At this time, an ordinary water supply might have quenched the flames, but none was at hand. Soon the flames were out of control and many buildings doomed to destruction. In all, there were twenty-six buildings destroyed: three hotels, sixteen stores, six barns, one warehouse, and the Tammany Hall residence.

The burned district covered the central and most prominent block in the village. The block was 375 feet long and 370 feet wide, with an alley running east and west. Every lot on that street was built upon, while the rear of the block had only four buildings.[8]

This was a major tragedy for the town and locals talked about it for months, believing Rose's spirit had reached out from beyond the grave, reminding all those who sent him to the gallows, that vengeance is the Lord's.

CHAPTER TWENTY-SEVEN
Rose's Spirit Seeks Justice

The life of any one man, however great, counts for very little in the course of affairs, and when he dies, the world goes on very much as it did while he was playing his part or before he was born.

The life of a man like William Rose probably counts for still less; whether he died innocent or guilty, his death makes no difference, but the sickening details in the manner of his execution have been documented and will never be repeated.[1]

The resolute courage and stoicism of Rose, who met his death at the gallows, elicited a kind of admiration for him, and he was regarded by many as a hero, rather than a villain.

Rose and his death will be remembered, as these events brought home to the people of Minnesota the truth that the prevailing system during the 1800s, of executing criminals, was radically, morally, and terribly wrong. The State of Minnesota finally abolished capital punishment in 1911, making it one of twelve states, and the District of Columbia, where crimes are not punishable by death.

❦

William Rose's spirit continues to seek justice and his words still ring loud and clear -- *I am innocent and some day the world may know it. I warn you, one and all, to watch the man I have spoken of and the time will come when you will all be convinced of his guilt as I am.*[2]

Someday, the final chapter in this saga will be written, when the truth will be revealed. Stories and diaries, commonly passed on to family descendants and local residents of the time, are locked away in an old trunk, in a dark, dusty attic somewhere, and will one day be discovered to provide the missing piece to what really happened one, hot August night in 1888. Only then will William Rose's fateful words be forever silenced, and his spirit rest in peace.

Author's Note

The characters in this book are real, and much of the story is in their own words based on newspaper reports, court documents, and personal stories. This is a work of nonfiction, and my intention has been to remain faithful to the characters and to the sequence of events as they actually happened. The interpretations of the characters are my own and some dialogue and scenes were created as a way to develop the characters' personality, temperament, or idiosyncrasies.

This book was written to document a very important part of Redwood County history, along with the surrounding counties in southwestern Minnesota, and to bring William Rose's tragic story to life. It is my hope that one day we may find justice for Rose, if in fact he was an innocent man wrongfully convicted. The writer believes there is someone out there who has the missing piece of information or evidence that could possibly clear an innocent man of this horrible crime and restore his family's good name. I hope they will have the courage to come forward to set the record straight, and solve this 120-year-old mystery of who really murdered Moses Lufkin. Justice delayed is not justice denied.

If anyone has substantial proof, information, or documentation related to this case that could bring justice for William Rose, please contact the author by mail: PO Box 52, Belview, MN 56214.

Notes

INTRODUCTION

1. Homestead Act - *www.archives.gov/homestead-act*
2. Timber Culture Act - *En.wikepedia.org/wiki/timber_culture_act*
3. Facts about Life on a farm in the 1800s, Sources: "America's Women, 400 Years of Dolls, Drudges, Helpmates and Heroines" by Gail Collins, - *http://answers.yahoo.com*

1 THE LUFKIN FAMILY

1. Letter written by Frances Lufkin, source unknown.
2. Whitman's Drum Taps and Washington's Civil War Hospitals by Angel Price, *http://xroads.virginia.edu/~CAP/hospital/Whitman.htm*
3. Divorce papers - Moses Lufkin, 1863, source unknown.

5 MINNIE MARRIES

1. Information and photos provided by Steven Foster, great nephew of Frank Foster.

6 GRACE MEETS BARNEY

1. State of MN, County of Murray, District Court 13th Judicial Dist., Testimony of Grace Benjamin, pgs. 3-7 Grace D. Benjamin, Plaintiff vs. Barney B. Benjamin, Defendant, Filed October 22, 1887
2. State of MN, County of Murray, District Court 13th Judicial Dist., Affidavit for Appointment, pgs. 1-3, Grace D. Benjamin, Plaintiff vs. Barney B. Benjamin, Defendant, Filed April 14, 1887

8 INCEST TRIAL

1. State of MN against Moses L. Lufkin, County of Murray, Criminal Complaint, February 13, 1888 James Rose's testimony, pgs. 1-5

2. ibid. John Rose's testimony, pgs. 6-9

3. ibid. Moses Lufkin's testimony, pgs. 10-14

4. ibid. Grace Lufkin's testimony, pgs. 15-17

5. ibid. Hiram Lakin's testimony, pgs. 18-20

6. ibid. Grand Jury decision, April 20, 1888

9 SLANDER CASES

1. State of MN, County of Murray, 13th Judicial District, Moses Lufkin vs. Wesley & Rosanna Averill and James & Martha Rose, October 11, 1887, Wesley Averill's deposition dated April 17, 1888, pgs. 1-3

2. ibid. George Lufkin's deposition dated April 5, 1888, pgs. 1-4

3. ibid. Emma Manchester's deposition dated April 6, 1888, pgs. 3-5

4. ibid. Loretta Gray's deposition dated April 4, 1888, pgs. 1-4

5. ibid. Flora Woodruff's deposition dated April 4, 1888, pgs. 1-5

10 SHOT IN THE BACK

1. Testimony of witness, Eli Slover at Coroner's Inquest on August 23, 1888. State of MN, County of Redwood in the town of Gales by Coroner G.R. Pease.

2. ibid.

3. ibid.

11 THE ARREST

1. State of MN, County of Redwood, Ninth Judicial District State of MN, Plaintiff, vs. William Rose, Defendant, November 12, 1889, Vol. III From William Rose's testimony, pg. 675

12 CORONER'S INQUEST

1. State of MN, County of Redwood, Ninth Judicial District State of MN, Plaintiff, vs. William Rose, Defendant, November 12, 1889, Vol. II From Dr. G.R. Pease testimony, pgs. 243-249

2. Coroner's Inquest, State of MN, County of Redwood, Town of Gales, August 23, 1888. From Eli Slover's Statement, pgs. 1-3

3. ibid.

4. "The Lufkin Murder." *The News Messenger* 7 September 1888: 4.

5. "More in Detail." *The Minneapolis Tribune* 17 October 1891: 1.

13 THE THIRD TRIAL

1. "Wm. Rose Guilty." *The News Messenger* 29 November 1889: 1.

2. "Convicted and Sentenced." *Redwood Reveille* 30 November 1889: 2.

3. State of MN, County of Redwood, Ninth Judicial District State of MN, Plaintiff, vs. William Rose, Defendant, November 12, 1889, Vol. I From Eli Slover's testimony starting on pg. 27.

4. State of MN, County of Redwood, Ninth Judicial District State of MN, Plaintiff, vs. William Rose, Defendant, November 12, 1889, Vol. III From Charles Anderson testimony starting on pg. 607-608.

5. State of MN, County of Redwood, Ninth Judicial District State of MN, Plaintiff, vs. William Rose, Defendant, November 12, 1889, Vol. III From James Rose testimony starting on pg. 763-765.

6. State of MN, Plaintiff, vs. William Rose, Defendant, November 12, 1889, Vol. II From Martha Rose testimony starting on pg. 427-428 and 457-460.

7. State of MN, County of Redwood, Ninth Judicial District State of MN, Plaintiff, vs. William Rose, Defendant, November 12, 1889, Vol. I From Eli Slover's testimony starting on pg. 27-110.

8. State of MN, County of Redwood, Ninth Judicial District State of MN, Plaintiff, vs. William Rose, Defendant, November 12, 1889, Vol. II From A.M. Grundin's testimony pgs. 340-341.

9. State of MN, County of Redwood, Ninth Judicial District State of MN, Plaintiff, vs. William Rose, Defendant, November 12, 1889, Vol. II From Joseph Aldrich's testimony pgs. 343-347.

10. State of MN, County of Redwood, Ninth Judicial District State of MN, Plaintiff, vs. William Rose, Defendant, November 12, 1889, Vol. III From William Rose's testimony starting on pg. 627.

11. "Convicted and Sentenced." *Redwood Reveille* 30 November 1889: 2.

12. ibid.

13. ibid.

14. ibid.

14 STATE SUPREME COURT APPEAL

1. State of MN Respondent vs. William Rose, Appellant, April 28, 1891

15 U.S. SUPREME COURT APPEAL

1. "Will Rose Hang?" *The News Messenger,* 1891

2. "Holden Must Hang." *The News Messenger* 12 December 1890: 1.

3. "Depends on Governor Bill." *New Ulm Review* 3 August 1891: 1.

4. "Mercy for William Rose." *New Ulm Review* 26 August 1891: 4.

5. ibid.

6. ibid.

7. ibid.

8. "Will Rose Hang?" *The News Messenger* 1891

16 NO FEAR OF DEATH

1. "Prepared to Sprout Wings." *New Ulm Review* 14 October 1891: 1.

2. "Rose Claims to be Innocent." *New Ulm Review* 14 October 1891: 1.

3. "His Plea for Life." *The Saint Paul Weekly Pioneer Press* 15 October 1891: 2.

4. ibid.

5. ibid.

6. "Merriam's Grit." *St. Paul Daily Globe* 16 October 1891: 2

17 LAST DAY IN NEW ULM

1. "His Last Day in New Ulm." *The Review* 21 October 1891: 2.

2. "He Sees a Clergyman." *St. Paul Daily Globe* 16 October 1891: 1.

3. "His Last Day in New Ulm." *The Review* 21 October 1891: 2.

4. "Rose is Interviewed." *St. Paul Daily Globe* 16 October 1891: 1.

5. ibid.

6. ibid.

7. ibid.

8. "A Victim of Jurisprudence." *Sleepy Eye Herald* 16 October 1891: 4.

9. ibid.

10. ibid.

18 LAST LETTER

1. "Rose's Last Letter." *Redwood Gazette* 22 October 1891: 4.

19 DEATH MARCH

1. "Bungling, Shocking." *St. Paul Daily Globe* 17 October 1891: 1.

2. ibid.

3. "More in Detail." *The Minneapolis Tribune* 17 October 1891: 1.

4. "Dropped to Death." *St. Paul Daily Globe* 16 October 1891: 1.

5. ibid.

20 THE HANGING

1. "Dropped to Death." *St. Paul Daily Globe* 16 October 1891: 1.

2. "Bungling, Shocking." *St. Paul Daily Globe* 17 October 1891: 1.

3. ibid.

4. "A Victim of Jurisprudence." *Sleepy Eye Herald* 16 October 1891: 4.

5. "More in Detail." *The Minneapolis Tribune* 17 October 1891: 1.

6. "Bungling, Shocking." *St. Paul Daily Globe* 17 October 1891: 1.

7. ibid.

8. "The Burial of William Rose." *Redwood Reveille* 24 October 1891: 2.

9. "Good-Bye to Rose." *Redwood Gazette* 22 October 1891: 4.

21 THE FUNERAL

1. "The Burial of William Rose." *Redwood Reveille* 24 October 1891: 2.

22 THE AFTERMATH

1. "Bungling, Shocking." *St. Paul Daily Globe* 17 October 1891: 1.
2. "Last Act in the Rose Tragedy." *Sleepy Eye Herald* 23 October 1891: 1.
3. "A Taste of Justice." *Redwood Gazette* 29, October 1891: 4.
4. "On Capital Punishment." *Redwood Gazette* 22 October 1891: 2.
5. ibid.
6. ibid.
7. ibid.
8. "A Taste of Justice." *Redwood Gazette* 29 October 1891: 4.

23 SLOVER'S STATEMENT

1. "Watch Slover." *Redwood Gazette* 22 October 1891: 2.
2. "Slover's Clean Record." *The News Messenger* 23 October 1891: 2.

24 WAS A CONFESSION MADE?

1. "Was a Confession Made." *Redwood Gazette* 24 January 1900: 1.
2. "No Confession Made." *Redwood Gazette* 31 January 1900: 2.
3. ibid.

25 OTHER POSSIBLE SUSPECTS

1. "In the Personal section." *Redwood Gazette* 29 October 1891: 4.

26 THE FATE OF THOSE LEFT BEHIND

1. *History of Redwood County*, compiled by Franklyn Curtiss-Wedge, 1916, pg. 467.
2. "Bright Jurist Suicide," from *www.footnote.com/image/92841864*
3. *Redwood the Story of a County*, by Wayne Webb, pgs. 488-489.
4. "Col. William Wallis Erwin Expired" *The Miami Metropolis* 14 September 1908

5. "Accident at the Illinois Central." *Champaign Daily News*, IL 10 November 1896

6. "A Shade of Romance." *The Minneapolis Tribune* 16 October 1891: 1.

7. "Aged Resident Passes Away; Funeral Sat." *Corning Observer*, CA 2 November 1934

8. "Disastrous Fire in Tracy."*The News Messenger* 4 December 1891: 1.

27 ROSE'S SPIRIT SEEKS JUSTICE
1. "The Execution of Rose." *St. Paul Daily Globe* 17 October 1891: 2.

2. "Bungling, Shocking." *St. Paul Daily Globe* 17 October 1891: 1.

CPSIA information can be obtained
at www.ICGtesting.com
Printed in the USA
FFOW05n1246240217

9 781432 791292